Rich by
Thirty

Rich by Thirty

A YOUNG ADULT'S GUIDE TO FINANCIAL SUCCESS

LESLEY SCORGIE

KEY PORTER BOOKS

Library and Archives Canada Cataloguing in Publication

Scorgie, Lesley
    Rich by thirty : a young adult's guide to financial success / Lesley Scorgie. — New US ed.

Includes index.
ISBN 978-1-55470-038-7

    1. Young adults—Finance, Personal.   2. Teenagers—Finance, Personal.   I. Title.

HG179.S353 2007A   332.0240084'2   C2007-904786-6

ONTARIO ARTS COUNCIL
CONSEIL DES ARTS DE L'ONTARIO

The publisher gratefully acknowledges the support of the Canada Council for the Arts and the Ontario Arts Council for its publishing program. We acknowledge the support of the Government of Ontario through the Ontario Media Development Corporation's Ontario Book Initiative.

We acknowledge the financial support of the Government of Canada through the Book Publishing Industry Development Program (BPIDP) for our publishing activities.

Key Porter Books Limited
Six Adelaide Street East, Tenth Floor
Toronto, Ontario
Canada M5C 1H6

www.keyporter.com

Distributed in the U.S. by Publishers Group West

www.pgw.com

Text design: Martin Gould
Electronic formatting: Jean Lightfoot Peters

Printed and bound in Canada

07 08 09 10 11 5 4 3 2 1

To my Grandmother Scorgie. Words cannot express how much your love, care, and influence have meant to me throughout the years. You're the greatest woman I've ever met—full of strength, courage, intelligence, beauty and support. I'm so blessed to have you in my life.

Acknowledgments

I would like to sincerely thank my family—Mom, Dad, Alison, and Stephen—for fuelling my life's ambitions with love and support. Thank you also to my extended family. You've cheered me on all the way to success. Thanks to my wonderful friends who have taught me how to love, laugh, cry, be strong, and, best of all, become me. Your inspiration and care over the years have been, and will continue to be, irreplaceable.

There are so many people who have taken time out of busy schedules to invest in and nurture my professional development. I want to thank those individuals who have guided me in my career and passions. Thanks to Claire for your perspective and energy. To my *Rich by Thirty* Web site and newsletter team, Erin and Marco: thanks for your exceptional efforts. We're making a difference! Finally, I want to thank Key Porter Books and KMLA for making my dreams of becoming an author come true.

Contents

Introduction

A few years ago, I met a woman whose story has stayed with me to this day. In fact, she's one of the reasons I decided to write this book. Mary was nearly seventy years old. She told me about the financial struggles and successes she'd experienced throughout her life. When she was young, she married and became pregnant. Her husband left her near the end of the pregnancy, taking the household savings with him. Mary was on her own—scared and expecting a new addition to her life.

Mary's son quickly became her reason to live and survive. Almost immediately after his birth, she had to find a job. After all, no one else was going to support them! With few family members or friends nearby, Mary relied on kind neighbors to look after the baby while she filed books at the local library. Money from her paychecks evaporated within days of receiving them.

Mary learned how to live a frugal life. She planned and documented her spending, so she could provide for the needs of her small family. Only the basics were affordable. There was no money left over for saving, trips, books, or entertainment. After a few years of living paycheck-to-paycheck, Mary was feeling defeated. She felt she was getting nowhere. Yes, she and her son were surviving, but questions were running around in her head. How could she get ahead financially, when she was barely making minimum wage? Would she ever be able to afford a home in a safe neighborhood, where her son could play outside? What about retirement? What would happen if her son wanted to go to college? What if she lost her job? Would she be able to pay the bills?

When the questions became too many to bear, Mary decided to take control. She borrowed money-management books from the library, talked to friends and family, and saw a financial adviser for the first time. She worked out a long-term financial strategy focused on saving what little she did have. She decided it was the only way she would feel secure and the only solution she could find to her financial problems.

Mary was only twenty-three years old when she made that decision—the decision to take control of her financial life. When Mary retired at the age of sixty-five, she owned a modest home with no mortgage and a fuel-efficient vehicle. Her son had graduated from college with her help and, better still, Mary had more than $650,000 in retirement savings!

Have you ever felt like Mary did, in the early years with her son? Have you ever felt saving money was something you'd never be able to do? Have you ever felt you'll never get ahead? Have you ever wanted something so badly, yet not been able to afford it? We've all had these feelings! But, like Mary, you can take control of the situation and learn how to overcome your particular obstacles. Whether you're in a situation like Mary and her son, or you just want to put some money away for a rainy day, the financial fundamentals you'll find in this book will see you through to a very wealthy life—in more ways than one.

Why Listen to Me?

Before you read any further, you'd probably like to know a little more about me. Who am I, and why am I telling you how to manage your money? Good questions!

I was born in Toronto, Ontario, Canada, in 1983 into an average family. My mom stayed at home until I was four years old, and my dad worked as a paramedic. When I was eight, my family moved out west to Edmonton, Alberta, so both my parents could go back to school and upgrade their education. As you can imagine, with both my parents in school, money was very tight. When they graduated in 1998, my family moved again—this time to Calgary, Alberta, so my parents could look for work in their respective fields. For the next four years, my family struggled with job stability and finances.

I didn't grow up in a wealthy home. Far from it. There were years in the mid-nineties when my family survived on $24,000 a year. That managed to feed and clothe five people, pay a small mortgage, pay parental tuition, and maintain one vehicle. For more than ten years, we had very small Christmas gifts, generic-brand food, and no lavish vacations. My brother, sister, and I relied on secondhand stores for our bicycles, clothing, and toys. There was no money to spare. During that time, I learned to live the frugal life. My entire family would look for deals, sales, and giveaways. We never paid full price for anything!

It's not hard to figure out my interest in money was sparked by the lack of it in my own home. Even at an early age, I'd carry around my piggy bank and inquire about the different coins I'd collected and what I could buy with them. My parents kindly answered most of my money questions, even though they were drowning in debt and bills. They also encouraged me to read up on my interest. Soon, I began to flip through *Forbes* and *Fortune* magazines. I picked my way through various articles and understood at least some of what I read. While I was reading about stock picking and entrepreneurial endeavors, my best friends were watching *Mighty Morphin Power Rangers*. I joined them on occasion, but more often than not, I fell deeper into my own interests.

As early as eight, I was operating a lemonade stand during the summer months and shoveling snow during the winter. I wanted to earn enough money for a trip to the pool, a visit to the candy store, or an outing to a movie. I set my sights, knew my targets, and went for it. As time passed, my initial motivations for saving and investing evolved from "making enough to go to the movies" to "making enough to retire with millions."

On my tenth birthday, with $100 of gift money, I purchased my first Government Savings Bond. My mom believed it was a great idea for me to learn first-hand what investing money was all about. From that time on, I bought more bonds every chance I could.

When I turned fourteen, I started working at the local public library. Not only did it earn me a small income, it gave me the chance to learn more about growing money through the books and newspapers I found on the shelves. I took it upon myself to investigate options for investing my money. I bought my first mutual funds that same year, and began investing in the stock market four years later, when I was eighteen. Once I started to see the growth in my own accounts—the power of compound interest—I was hooked!

From Frugal to Extraordinary: The Oprah Experience

In eleventh grade, my management and marketing class was learning about investing. My teacher was having difficulty explaining the concept to our class because my peers were totally unresponsive. One day, in complete frustration, she asked if any student would like to try teaching this part of the course. I raised my hand, and away I went.

I took a few class periods to share my knowledge with my friends. It just so happened, during the same week, a local newspaper phoned the school to ask if there were any "odd or interesting" students they could profile. I was nominated due to my financial knowledge. The newspaper agreed I fit the criteria—I hoped I was more interesting than odd!—and they went ahead with the interview. They published a front-page article entitled "Whiz Kid" and then posted it on the Internet.

In February 2001, I received a phone call from a producer at *The Oprah Winfrey Show*. She had seen the article on the Internet and wanted to talk about my investment and money-management savvy. Two weeks later, I was on the show!

The theme was "Ordinary People, Extraordinary Wealth." I was one of a few guests sharing their financial savvy and secrets with more than twenty million viewers! What set me apart from the others? I was the only guest under the age of forty. I was there to demonstrate that you can have a very typical young life and still make positive financial choices.

Since being on *Oprah*, I've completed my Bachelor of Commerce degree in finance and marketing, and written for a number of newspapers and magazines. I'm now twenty-four years old. I own a house, have a good job, and savings for the future. I also have a lot of fun! By the time I retire, I'll have millions of dollars in savings and assets. Because of this success, I've become a spokesperson and advocate for young people who want to chase their dreams, and be fully equipped to handle the price tag. My passion is for teaching and speaking about money management and financial literacy. I've delivered presentations to thousands of people across North America, with audiences ranging in age from six to eighty.

Before we go any further, I want to assure you I was (and still am!) totally normal—like you! I went to school, worked a part-time job through high school and university, and completed my homework even when it was tough or boring. On weekends, I socialized with friends and squeezed in a little relaxing time. I went through the same ups and downs every young person experiences. The only difference? I wanted to be wealthy by the time I was thirty and so I started planning earlier than usual to make that happen.

Listen Up!

Out of all the advice you'll read in the following pages, this could be the most important: "normal" lives can lead to extraordinary accomplishments. You may think you can't do this, or what little you have to contribute to your own financial future isn't enough. But you can, and it is. All of your time, talent, money, and effort will pay off in the long run, if you can focus on making some positive choices. My own financial choices have led me to a point where I'll have millions of dollars upon retirement. And the best part is I haven't had to make huge sacrifices to get there.

So how do you do it? This book is going to get you started. As you read, you'll find useful information about getting motivated and organized, getting smart with your money, and getting started with your savings and investing. Perhaps for the first time in your life, you'll be getting financial advice from someone your own age—someone like you. You'll learn basic money management, including how to make or find money, debt reduction, budgeting, and investment strategies. You'll learn how to live a frugal life without making painful sacrifices. You'll learn why it makes so much sense to start planning when you're young, and why it pays to diversify. You'll learn the difference between savings and investing, and pick up some short- and long-term investing strategies. Perhaps most importantly, you'll learn that money is only one part of a balanced and happy life.

When the tips, techniques, and strategies on the following pages are combined, they make for a very rich lifestyle and great personal and financial fulfillment. This book doesn't offer a "get-rich-quick" scheme. It's about learning the financial fundamentals to secure your financial future in the long term. And, by reading this book, you're well on your way to financial success.

1

Get Motivated:

WHY MONEY MATTERS

It's not all about the money. At least, that's what study results are telling us. These days, North Americans under thirty don't care about money nearly as much as previous generations did. These days, we're looking for balance and personal fulfillment. We seek opportunities for growth, flexibility, and fun in our professional and personal lives. And we're well aware money doesn't necessarily provide all of the above.

On one hand, I think it's fantastic our generation is willing to separate the pursuit of happiness from monetary success. On the other, I truly believe not caring about money is a big mistake! Being smart about your money—how you spend it, how you manage it—can make a huge difference in the quality of your life. It can open doors, or close them. It can help you realize your goals and dreams, or ensure you won't.

A Few Boring Truths

Ready or not, the future is upon you. Before you even know it, you'll be thinking about things like the cost of post-secondary education, mortgages, cars, kids, vacations, and—yup—retirement! It may sound boring, but it's your responsibility to think about these things. You must take positive steps now, so you can create the future you want. You're the only one who can make your own dreams—financial and otherwise—come true. If you don't look out for your future, who will?

The Sort-of-Boring Truth about the Distant Future

Kevin is twenty-three years old, and the youngest of three children in his family. His mom and dad are both in their mid-sixties, but neither one can afford to retire. The situation is starting to worry Kevin. His parents seem tired all the time, and he's concerned about their health. He's even started to take on extra shifts at work, so he can help out with the bills and the groceries. One thing Kevin knows for sure is he doesn't want to end up in the same position when he turns sixty! He knows the only way to avoid this scenario is to work hard now, and get smart with his money.

Money is the key to your long-term financial security. It's scary to think about this, but by the time you're ready to retire, you will need approximately four times the amount of money you need now—just to live the way you're living now (keep those "lifestyles of the rich and famous" fantasies in check!). This hard-to-swallow truth is due to a nasty little thing called inflation. Inflation makes the dollars in your bank account today less powerful as time goes by. For example, $4 today might only be worth $1 forty years from now.

Think about it this way: a sixty-five-year-old woman with $1 million in retirement savings could call it quits tomorrow and not have to live below the poverty line. However, forty years from now, a sixty-five-year-old woman wanting to call it quits would need to have socked away $4 million to maintain her lifestyle! Another way to look at it is $1 million today will be worth only $250,000 (approximately) in forty years.

If this isn't scary or depressing enough, wait until you hear the next part! The next time you receive a paycheck, have a look at the section on the stub where the deductions are listed. There are deductions for income tax, social security, and maybe other things, like Medicare and Unemployment Insurance. On average, for every dollar you earn, you're really only taking home seventy cents and, sometimes, less. What it boils down to is you end up paying Uncle Sam before anyone else, including yourself—the one who earned the paycheck in the first place.

At the end of the day, the government helps you out with your retirement savings to a small degree, through a program called Social Security. But this government savings plan will not allow you to retire comfortably. We'll more likely have to count on ourselves to maintain our financial security. Boring, and a little bit depressing, but true.

So, your money becomes less and less powerful and valuable as time passes. And you're not likely to get much help from the government, or anyone else, for that matter. Are you ever going to be able to retire? Or buy a house? Or go on vacation? Of course you will—if you learn to care about your money. Handled properly and managed wisely, your money can not only keep up with inflation, it can beat it!

The Not-So-Boring Truth about the Not-So-Distant Future

Maya is sixteen years old and in her junior year of high school. She has average grades and comes from a financially average household. She loves to hang out with her friends, dance, and, most importantly—shop!

Recently, Maya has started to think about what she might want to do with her life. She made an appointment with the guidance counselor at school to discuss her dream of becoming a doctor. When she sat down with the counselor, however, she discovered two things: the cost of medical school was very high, and her grades would also have to be very high to have any chance of getting a scholarship. Now, Maya's reconsidering. Unless something changes—both with her commitment to school, and her financial planning—her dream will never become a reality.

If you were drifting off during the last section—or, at least, wondering why you need to think about retirement when you're still in your teens or twenties—maybe this section will hit home a little harder. You need to care about your money because, even though you're young, money still affects you. In fact, money affects everyone.

What do you want to do with your life? Do you want to be a pilot? A nurse? A musician? You'll need money to do it. Money is also necessary if you want to go snowboarding, buy a home, travel, or shop.

It comes down to this: money enables us to have more choices. The more we understand it—how to make it, how to save and invest it, how to spend it wisely—the more freedom we'll have. Think about what your life would be like if you didn't have enough money to go to a movie with a friend. Think about how frustrated you would be if you really wanted to become a doctor, but couldn't afford the tuition fees. The more financial freedom you have, the more freedom you'll have in all areas of your life. You'll be free to make choices best suited to your needs and goals. And isn't that what everyone wants?

THE $5,000 QUESTION

If you came home to find a check for $5,000 in your mailbox, what would you do with it? Would you save the money, buy a car, some clothes, or a hot new sound system? Would you give some to charity, pay off a loan, or take your friends out for a fabulous dinner? It's nice to have so many options, isn't it?

Now consider the opposite situation. Your most recent shopping trip got a little out of hand and you're looking at a $5,000 credit card bill! What are your options now? Remember, money leads to choices, and choices lead to freedom.

The Not-So-Boring Truth about Time

I know, I know. All this stuff about retirement and choices and freedom makes perfect sense to you, but still... You're probably scratching your head right now, trying to figure out how you—an average person under thirty, with hardly any disposable income—are supposed to take control of your financial life when some fifty and sixty year olds haven't gotten the hang of it yet. They have good jobs, houses, and lots of other stuff you don't have, right? That's true. But you have one thing they don't have, and it may be the most important thing of all: time.

Time is a pretty handy thing to have on your side. With time, you can grow your money substantially, without doing nearly as much work as you might expect. You can do this through the power of compound interest.

Imagine yourself at the top of a hill, making a snowball. It's a nice, round snowball taking you all of thirty seconds to make. When you aren't looking, the wind blows the snowball down the hill. As it's rolling, it picks up more and more snow until, a couple of minutes later and with no additional help from you, a giant snowball stops at the bottom of the hill. That's how compound interest works. You earn interest on your initial investment, which is then reinvested, allowing you to earn interest on it, as well. So now you're earning interest on your interest. As time passes, your growth "snowballs" into something quite impressive.

The chart on page 25 is an abbreviated version of one you'll see in chapter 6. For now, all you need to know is if you start early enough, and contribute to an investment plan regularly—increasing your contribution levels as you advance in your life and career—you can turn yourself into a millionaire by starting with as little as $35 a month and stopping your contributions after the age of 45, as I did in this example. (These results are based on generating an 8.5 percent return on your investments.)

The Power of Compound Interest

AGE	SAVED PER MONTH	TOTAL SAVED (WITH COMPOUND INTEREST)
16	$35	$455.70
23	$150	$6,432.82
30	$250	$30,384.16
40	$350	$118,288.33
45*	stop contributing after 45	$204,866.97
65		$1,047,289.39

Impressive, isn't it? If the chart isn't enough to inspire you, think about it this way: you can actually *double* your money with the power of compound interest. I'd like to introduce you to what investment types call the Rule of 72. Basically, if your investments are earning a return of 10 percent, you will double your money every 7.2 years. Here's how the formula works:

Time it will take for your money to double = 72/rate of return

So, if you keep your money in a growth-oriented portfolio (more on that in chapter 7) averaging a 12 percent rate of return, it will take six years for your money to double ($72/12 = 6$). On the other hand, if your ordinary savings account is earning 2 percent, you're looking at thirty-six years to double your money! See what a difference interest can make?

* Technically, you *could* stop making your monthly contribution after 45. However, I would recommend continuing to save. It will increase your financial freedom and flexibility.

Making It Personal

I'm hoping, by now, you've developed a greater appreciation of what money can do for you—how you can make it work to your advantage, how it can change your life for the better. I'm also hoping you're sufficiently motivated to dive in and get started. It's never too early (or too late) to take control of your financial future.

Goals Lead and Dreams Follow

Do you have dreams and goals? Of course you do! Have you ever wanted something so badly you simply had to find a way to get it? Throughout my university years, I dreamed about having my own place when I graduated. For four years, I saved a little money each month so I'd have enough for a small down payment on a townhouse upon graduation. My goal of owning a place led me to take actions to make it happen. Now my dream of owning a home has come true.

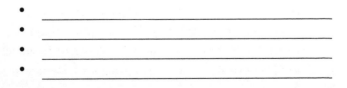

Goals ⟶ Actions ⟶ Dreams

Goals don't have to be huge to be real. Your goal could be to buy a bike next year. Or you may want to complete your post-secondary education with no student debt. To set goals, you must look into your future and figure out where you want to go, and what you want to do and have.

What are some of your financial goals?

- _____
- _____
- _____
- _____

This goal business can be tricky. Some goals, like saving for a computer or a car, make perfect sense. Others, like winning the lottery and retiring to Hawaii at the age of twenty-five, may not be so practical. When you set your goals, there are a few things you can do to make sure they have a real chance of happening.

- **Think short and long term:** Sometimes it can take years to have a clear idea of where you want to go, especially when it comes to your money. What do you see for yourself in the future? In particular, how much money do you want to have saved up in one year? In three years? In ten years? In fifty years? What do you want to be doing in those same time periods? Jot down your thoughts in the chart below. Committing your goals to paper is like developing a contract with yourself—one only you can accomplish or break. People who write down their goals are more likely to achieve them than people who don't.

TIME FRAME	PERSONAL GOALS	FINANCIAL GOALS
One year		
Three years		
Ten years		
Fifty years		

- **Create SMART goals:** smart goals are Specific, Measurable, Attainable, Realistic, and Timely. Rather than writing down a goal stating, "I want to be a millionaire," you might try this: "I want to have $1 million by the time I'm sixty-five, using the financial fundamentals and investing techniques I learned in

Rich by Thirty." That goal is much clearer than the first, and it has all of the elements of a smart goal. Look at the goals you wrote down on page 26 and in the chart above. Do any of them need to be revised? If so, do that here:

- _____
- _____
- _____
- _____

- **Create a personal vision statement:** Writing a personal vision statement is a huge step toward personal financial success. A vision statement includes both what you want to do in your life and how you are going to do it. A good vision statement will include the following:

  - Who (you!)
  - What (the goal)
  - When (the time frame)
  - How (the action plan)

One of the goals mentioned above was "I want to have $1 million by the time I'm sixty-five, using the financial fundamentals and investing techniques I learned in *Rich by Thirty*." Here is an example of a personal vision statement to support that goal:

I, Jane Smith, want to accomplish financial success (over $1 million) by retirement using financial fundamentals that include spending wisely, saving and investing, and giving back to the community.

Writing your personal vision statement can be challenging. Sometimes it's difficult to know where we really want to go in the long term. Most of us, though, have at least some sort of idea. Give it a whirl, and don't worry if it takes a couple of tries to get it right.

_____

_____

_____

_____

If you've got a computer at home, type your vision statement into a program and design a certificate around it. Print it off and frame it. Hang it on your wall so, whenever you see it, you're reminded of the positive direction in which you're headed.

I use my personal vision statement as a reminder of what I want to do with my life. But, as time passes and I change, so do my goals and visions. Don't feel too boxed in by one statement or one set of goals. Make changes to your vision as it becomes clearer through time.

EXCUSES, EXCUSES!

What's holding you back? Make a list of all the reasons you don't think you can get your finances in order. Then, put it somewhere safe and be prepared to tear it up in the not-so-distant future. Once you get through the next several chapters, you won't need it anymore, because you'll be on your way. Nothing will hold you back!

Hopefully, you're feeling a little more inspired and motivated than you were when you started reading this book. You know how important it is to start working on your financial future as early as possible, and you know how integral money can be to your future—both short and long term. Now you're ready to put the wheels in motion. You're ready to go out and make it happen!

2
Get Organized:
FILE FOLDERS, BANKS, AND YOU

Organization truly *is* the key to success. In fact, on the road to wealth and splendor, getting organized is the most important step you'll need to take. This process is often referred to as "getting your financial house in order." It may sound a little intimidating, but it's not. It can actually be fun.

The Tools of the Trade

Meet Erica, age twenty-six. She works full-time and rents a small apartment with a roommate. Unfortunately for both of them, Erica has never been very good at managing her money. She never knows how much money she has in her checking or savings accounts, and her cell phone bills and credit card bills are always stuffed inside her purse or in the glove compartment of her car. Often, her debit/ATM card and credit cards are declined at stores. Erica jokes with her friends she never knows when her bills are due until her phone service is cut off.

This is funny enough, until she gets stuck on the highway with a broken-down car and no cell phone service to enable her to call for help!

Erica needs to get organized! If you read the last paragraph with a sinking feeling in the pit of your stomach, don't worry. It's never too late to start!

File Folders Are Your Friends!

The very first step in your organization process should be a trip to the local office-supply store. Head straight to the file-folder aisle and start shopping. You'll need some multicolored file folders, and something to keep them in (an accordion case, or one of those desktop hanging-folder contraptions will do the trick).

Files are important because they allow you to separate and manage all the paperwork pertaining to the different areas of your financial and personal life. Filing also gives you an opportunity to review your financial and personal information more carefully.

Here are some examples of file names that might be relevant for you:

- bank statements (if you have more than one account, make a file for each, and include the account number or type on the tab for easy reference)
- utility bills (again, one folder for each utility)
- cell phone bills
- receipts
- credit card bills and related materials
- pay statements/employment information
- tax/government-related materials

- investment statements
- investment information
- health information
- certificates of achievement
- school information

This should be enough to get you started. As you start going through the stacks of important papers in your dresser drawers or on your desk, you'll probably find other materials that should also be given a file. Don't get carried away! You don't need to file *every* piece of paper making its way into your home. A rule of thumb: only file things that are important to you and could significantly affect your life.

When you organize your brand-new files, put them into an order that makes sense to you—alphabetical, most frequently used, whatever. Just choose a system that will allow you to easily remember where things go.

The Dreaded Spreadsheet

Although some people run screaming at the thought, a truly great way to get organized with your finances is to set up budgets using a computerized spreadsheet program (there will be a lot more information on budgets in chapter 3). Most software packages come with a basic spreadsheet program, and that's all you really need. It allows you to insert formulas to add and subtract numbers automatically, or dates to assist you in planning for certain purchases. I use Microsoft® Excel® to keep track of all my income and expenses.

You can also use your computer to create a list of "big-ticket items" you can work toward purchasing, as time progresses. For example, you could include items like a bicycle ($350), car repairs ($900), or a down payment on a new home ($5,000). Put your list someplace where you'll see it on a daily basis (I have mine taped to my desk at home). It will help to motivate you and keep you focused on your goals.

Let Technology Work for You

Getting organized with your investments has become increasingly easier in recent years, thanks to huge advances in Internet technology. Now, all you have to do is log on for a few minutes to check your investments, your bank balances, pay your bills, whatever! Make sure you register for your bank's online services (you may need to see a customer service representative to do this). If you have started to invest, you can also use the Internet to track the performance of almost any stock, bond, or mutual fund. Two good Web sites are www.finance.yahoo.com and www.bloomberg.com. Most North American financial services companies, like where you do your banking, will have Web sites containing relevant financial information.

These Web sites, and others like them, include graphs showing the historical performance of your investment. They also include information to help you determine if a particular investment would be good for you. Some Web sites even allow you to download data for creating graphs in spreadsheet programs.

Ten Minutes a Week

Getting a handle on your money doesn't take much more than a little planning, and checking up once a week. If you're willing to take ten minutes out of your busy week to devote to your financial future, I can guarantee you success. How many hours a day do you spend watching television? If you are like most North Americans in our age group, you are glued to the tube for nearly 3.5 hours a day! That adds up to a stunning 24.5 hours per week!

What's your least favorite show? Can you turn it on ten minutes late, or, better yet, not watch it at all? If you can commit to that, you can spend the time doing something that will really benefit you in the long run. With the ten minutes you manage to free up, you could

- Review your banking transactions: This will help you keep track of your income and expenses to ensure you aren't overspending.
- Brush up on your investment skills: Read a book about money management, visit financial Web sites, read the newspaper!
- Keep tabs on how your investments are doing.
- Set up your automatic banking transactions for the coming week.

The Big, Bad Bank

Nineteen-year-old Kumar is in his second year of university. He hides half of his savings underneath the hard drive of his computer. The other half can be found in a small box in his closet. At any given time, he has a stash of more than $9,000 hiding in his room! Because he can easily access his own money, he considers this technique more financially convenient than a bank.

Despite often getting a bad rap, banks are not evil. In fact, a good relationship with a bank you're comfortable with is a key component in your getting-organized campaign—as important as those multicolored file folders I recommended above!

As convenient as it may seem to have money sitting under your hard drive, it isn't very safe. There are way too many risks associated with keeping your money "under your mattress," rather than in a bank account. What if your house was robbed? What if your roof leaked, or there was a fire? You could lose everything! Besides, if your money is sitting in your closet, it isn't earning interest, is it? And if you read chapter 1 carefully, you now know how important interest can be. The best place for your money is in an account where you can monitor its activity.

Setting up an Account

If you haven't already set up a bank account for yourself, now is the time. The first step is to pick a bank or institution you would like to deal with. Here is a list of the ten largest banks, according to total deposits, in the United States at the end of June 2006:

- Bank of America Corp. (www.bankofamerica.com)
- J.P. Morgan Chase & Co. (www.jpmorganchase.com)
- Citigroup (www.citigroup.com)
- Wachovia Corp. (www.wachovia.com)
- Wells Fargo & Company (www.wellsfargo.com)
- Washington Mutual Bank (www.wamu.com)
- U.S. Bank (www.usbank.com)
- SunTrust Banks, Inc. (www.suntrust.com)
- HSBC Bank USA, N.A. (www.hsbcusa.com)
- World Savings (www.worldsavings.com)

You have a number of options when hunting around for a bank to deal with. There are even localized banks or institutions within your community. In addition to those, online banks like ING Direct (http://home.ingdirect.com) are becoming increasingly popular.

When selecting a bank, consider location, convenience, policy, and customer service. Check out their Web sites using the Internet and pay attention to word-of-mouth reputation.

Once you've selected the institution you'd like to deal with, it's time to set up your accounts. If you are under eighteen, you may need to bring a parent or guardian along. You'll also need at least two pieces of up-to-date identification (a driver's license, birth certificate, passport, or Social Security card, for example). Finally, be aware some financial institutions require a minimum deposit of up to $100 on the day you open your account. Once you have all that in order, an account representative or financial adviser will help you to determine what type of account will best suit your needs.

CHECKING ACCOUNTS A checking account is designed for activity. Typically, people have their paychecks deposited into it and pay their bills and spend out of it. As the name suggests, you are also able to write checks on it. A checking account generally doesn't receive any deposit interest, which makes it less than ideal for long-term savings. Use a checking account only if you are likely to spend your money within two months.

Because of the activity associated with checking accounts, there is usually a service fee to be paid. While I was a student, I had to pay $3.50 each month to use my account. That banking package gave me twenty-five transactions per month, and free online banking. Now, I'm working full time, and I pay $12 per month for my checking account. For that, I get sixty-five transactions per month, free online banking, and new checks when I need them. This usually meets my needs. It's worthwhile looking into these packages when opening an account. Otherwise, you might find yourself paying some hefty fees (up to $1 per transaction)! You can find information about banking packages online, or by calling your bank's toll-free customer service number.

SAVINGS ACCOUNTS A savings account is designed as a place you can park your money for a longer period of time. You receive interest on the money you have sitting in this account, but it isn't very much. Generally, it's worth thinking of your savings account as a place to put money you'll have for between two months and one year. For example, I save money for my yearly holidays in a savings account, but I don't put my retirement savings there. Savings accounts usually only have service fees if you use them actively to withdraw money. This is to hinder you from spending your savings. The fees can be higher than in the checking account (up to $3 per transaction), making it worth your while not to pull money out too frequently.

I highly recommend you open both a checking and a savings account. It's almost impossible to save for the long term in the same account you use for daily banking activity. Separating your money will make your financial life much easier (you won't accidentally spend your savings!), and help you develop healthy financial habits.

DEBIT/ATM CARDS AND ONLINE/TELEPHONE ACCESS When you're in the process of opening your checking and savings accounts, think about whether you want or need a debit card/ATM card. This card allows you to pay for your purchases directly at the stores where you shop, and gives you ATM access to your various accounts. It also makes online and telephone banking possible. Debit/ATM cards can be wonderfully convenient. Unfortunately, they can also tempt you to spend too much money.

If you're given a choice, I'd recommend getting a card allowing access to your checking account but not your savings account. This way, you'll have the convenience of accessing your money when you need it, but you won't end up touching your savings. As your comfort level with money increases, you might want to consider allowing yourself access to your savings, but only for the purpose of direct deposits and emergencies.

Lastly, ensure you have access to online- and telephone-banking services. They're invaluable tools when it comes to automating your investment services.

A BANKING CHECKLIST Here's a quick "to do" list to keep in mind when opening your accounts:

- Choose a bank or institution to suit your needs.
- Make an appointment with a financial adviser ahead of time.
- Bring along your mom, dad, or a legal guardian (if under eighteen).
- Bring at least two pieces of current identification.
- Ask to open both a checking and a savings account.

- Research your bank's service packages, and find the one that works for you.
- Be prepared to make a minimum deposit.
- Get a debit/ATM card and set it up with access to your checking account only.
- Set up online and telephone banking.

BUYER BEWARE!

When you visit the bank to open your new accounts, don't be surprised if the financial adviser tries to sell you a credit card. Avoid the temptation to sign up—at least for now. You'll find a lot more information on credit in chapter 4.

Fees, Fees, and More Fees

Many people go ballistic over the service fees they pay to their banks. Maybe it's because we all know how much money banks are raking in. Let's face it—at least some of that profit is coming out of your account, if not via fees, then through the interest they earn by using your money for their own investments.

It's worth keeping in mind, though, the fees you pay don't buy a physical product. They buy a service. After all, financial institutions have to staff their various departments in order to serve you and their other clients. They transfer a portion of that cost down to you. Banks providing a high level of customer service tend to charge higher fees; those operating on more of a self-serve basis charge less.

To get a clear picture of how this works, let's compare ING Direct to Bank of America. When you have a savings account with ING Direct, an online banking institution, there are far fewer people to serve you because they have fewer branch locations. There is limited "service" available, except by phone and online, therefore, there are few service fees. In fact, ING Direct typically doesn't charge you fees on something like your savings account. On the other hand, Bank of America offers teller services, as well as many other account services. You could, for example, meet with someone to talk specifically about your debit/ATM card limits, loans, mortgages, or investments. You can talk to a representative if and when you want. Not surprisingly, this service costs money.

A similar situation exists with brokerage or trading accounts. Let's say you're a very confident investor, and you've been investing in the stock market for many years. You make your own investment decisions without the influence of your broker or financial planner. You don't need, or want, to pay for their advice. You'd be best served by an online-trading account allowing you to trade what, when, and where you want, all for as low as $9.99 per transaction. However, an investor who doesn't want the hassle, has less knowledge, etc., might prefer to use a full-service broker, regardless of the fee (which can be a percentage of total funds invested or upwards of $300 per transaction).

In the end, how you feel about service fees will likely depend on your priorities. Do you value high customer-service levels? If you do chose to go with a bank that charges service fees, make sure you're getting good service for your money. If, at any time, you feel you're being let down by the customer service representatives, feel free to speak up. The consumer—regardless of his or her age—is very powerful! Good institutions will recognize and respect that. People in the banking services industry should want to help guide young customers down the path of financial security. If they aren't willing to support you in your banking and investing endeavors, they don't deserve your business.

Advisers and Other Bankers

When you arrive at whichever financial institution you've chosen, a financial adviser will assist you in setting up your accounts. Financial advisers can handle most non-transaction account services. For example, they can assist in choosing and setting up the best accounts for your needs, selecting the proper service-fee package, and setting up your debit/ATM card. Often, financial advisers will also be able to set up basic investments. They can ask you questions about your long-term and short-term goals to help determine what basic investments will suit your needs.

By the time you're finished this book, you'll likely be able to start putting together your own financial plan, without the help of an adviser. However, when you've got a good handle on the basics, it's great to get some advice. Financial advisers often share good ideas for your money, and the more information you have, the better. They also tend to approach your personal money management in a very organized manner. Knowledge is a very powerful tool. I highly recommend sitting down with a financial adviser to work out a plan that works for you.

GET A JOB!
So, we've been talking about getting organized and about banking. But, what if you don't have any money coming in? The only real way to make money

is to work for it, or make it work for you. If you don't have an income stream, it's definitely time to get one. Traditionally, we think about working a "regular" job as a means to make money. However, you can think about making money in a variety of ways. Here are a few things you can do:

- Start your own small business
- Trade things on eBay for a profit
- Baby-sit
- Tutor
- Freelance your services
- Get a job in your field of interest
- Get creative with your investments

If you choose the more traditional path of job hunting, I have a few recommendations: try to work in a field that interests you—you don't want to get yourself into a job you hate doing; spice up your résumé and cover letters, and customize them to suit the job you're looking for; read up on proper interviewing and networking techniques. Finally, use all the job-hunting resources out there. Online job-search engines like Monster (www.monster.com), Career Builder (www.careerbuilder.com), or JobBank USA (www.jobbankusa.com) will assist you in developing your résumé and cover letter. They also feature many job postings. Some even provide information to help you determine what career opportunities would be a good match for your skill set and personality.

3

Get Started:

THE JOYS OF BUDGETING

Now that you're organized (or at least, on your way to being organized), it's time to start properly managing your money. And the first step in this process is a budget. Unfortunately, budgets have a bad reputation—they're boring, they take a lot of time, they're restricting, etc.

Yup, I'd be in denial if I didn't admit a lot of people—especially people our age—don't like to think about budgets. Yes, I understand the whole idea is kind of boring, and it does seem to suggest huge compromises will need to be made regarding your spending. Well, that second part may be partially true (small compromises will likely need to be made), but budgeting isn't boring; it's essential. A good budget is a vital first step on the road to financial success. Without one, it's next to impossible to know where your money is coming from, or where it's going to. But preparing a budget isn't difficult, and you can think of the exercise as very little pain now for a whole lot of gain later.

DON'T BE LATE!
The only time developing a budget can get tricky is if you do it too late. Let's say you're on a road trip with your friends. You drive for five hours and arrive at the hotel. You pay for the room, go out for a fancy dinner, do some shopping, and put a little more gas in the car. As you merrily spend away, no one stops to think about how much money is left in the "bank." What happens the next day when the car breaks down and you realize you've only got a little cash left? You can avoid this situation by creating a simple budget, and sticking to it, before you start any adventure.

The 411 on Budgeting

A budget is a financial statement or document outlining your income and expenditures over a specific period of time. Think of it as a plan for your money—and remember it doesn't have to be complicated. All you really need to prepare a budget is the spreadsheet software that comes with your computer, or some graph paper. To prove just how easy it really is, we're going to walk through the creation of your own personal budget together.

Income and Expenses

First things first. Any budget—be it corporate, household, or personal—begins with an examination of income. Where's the money coming from? For corporations, answering this question can be an extremely complex exercise; for you, it shouldn't be very hard.

Below are a few examples of the "income" portion of a budget. First is the monthly budget of Noor, a seventeen-year-old high school student; second is the monthly budget of Peter, a twenty-five-year-old career person.

Noor (Student)

SOURCES OF INCOME	DOLLARS
Part-Time Job	500
Small Side Jobs	50
Total Income	**$550**

Peter (Young Career Person)

SOURCES OF INCOME	DOLLARS
Full-Time Job	2,800
Small Side Jobs	50
Total Income	**$2,850**

So far, so good. Now, think about your situation. Do you have a full- or part-time job? Do you earn an allowance for doing chores around the house? You need to take into account any money you have coming in. Now, fill in and total up the "income" portion of your own budget in the worksheet below, or in your spreadsheet program.

SOURCES OF INCOME	DOLLARS
Total Income	

Once you have your total income figured out, it's time to look at your expenses. What do you spend money on every month? Be really careful here. You need to think about everything—from big-picture stuff, like car loans and rent, to little things, like coffee and lunches in the school cafeteria. Keeping track of your expenses is the cornerstone of your financial well-being. One of the top reasons people (and businesses) go bankrupt is improper cash-flow management. Simply put, more money ends up going out than coming in. Not a good scene!

Let's get back to Noor and Peter and have a look at the expenditure portion of their budgets.

Noor (Student)

SOURCES OF EXPENSES	DOLLARS
Clothing	50
Food	50
Savings	50
Entertainment	100
School Expenses	150
Total Expenses	**$400**

Peter (Young Career Person)

SOURCES OF EXPENSES	DOLLARS
Mortgage or Rent	850
Loan	300
Credit Card Payment	125
Groceries	150
Investment Account	75
Heat	90
Property Tax	120
Electricity	55

Condo Fees	200
Home and Auto Insurance	125
Transit Tickets	70
Vehicle Fuel	120
Subtotal of Mandatory Expenses	**$2,280**
Bank Overdraft	400
Furniture Payment	100
Cell Phone Bill	65
Cable, Phone, Internet	125
Gym Membership	32
Subtotal of Secondary Expenses	**$722**
Fun Money	200
Subtotal of Fun Expenses	**$200**
Total Expenses	**$3,202**

A couple of notes on the categories in Peter's budget: Mandatory expenses are things you literally can't live without. You'll notice Peter's investments are in this category. Yes, your financial security is indeed that important. Secondary expenses, on the other hand, are things you could live without if push came to shove. They tend to be things we value, or things that make our lives a bit easier. The fun expenses category includes pure luxury items— things to make our lives more exciting.

Now it's your turn. Use the worksheet below to fill in your own monthly expenses.

SOURCES OF EXPENSES	DOLLARS
Total Expenses	

We're down to the final piece of the puzzle now—blending the income portion of your budget with the expense portion. Subtract the total expenses from the total income to see whether you have a net income or net loss. This depends on whether you spend less than you make (net income), or more (net loss). Here are Noor and Peter, continued:

Noor (Student)

Total Monthly Income	550
Total Monthly Expenses	400
Net Income or Loss	**$150**

Peter (Young Career Person)

Total Monthly Income	2,850
Total Monthly Expenses	3,202
Net Income or Loss	**$(352)**

Noor is doing very well. She's experiencing a net income of $150 every month. If she wants to save for something, or invest for the future, she knows exactly how much money she can use. Peter, on the other hand, isn't faring so well. He's looking at a net monthly loss of $352. Clearly, something's not working. After paying his mandatory expenses each month, there's hardly any money left over. This phenomenon is often called home poverty, and it's pretty common for young home owners or renters. To avoid this situation, lifestyle changes are likely needed—a roommate, perhaps, or a move to cheaper accommodations. There will be more information on how to handle this on page 61.

Now it's time to calculate your net income or loss. Fill in the worksheet below, and grab a calculator.

Total Monthly Income	
Total Monthly Expenses	
Net Income or Loss	

How did you do? Are you in a positive or negative position? Don't feel bad if your "bottom line" (now you know where that term comes from!) isn't looking great. You're certainly not alone, and part of the reason you bought this book was to help you get control of your financial life, right?

The bottom line of your budget should act as a guide for the next steps in your financial makeover. If the number is negative, you're overspending. In financial circles, this is referred to as a deficit, and to say it's generally frowned upon is an understatement. If, on the other hand, your bottom line is positive, you're in a surplus situation— all in all, a much happier place to be!

Surpluses are usually produced when a budget allots more money for a specific product or service than is actually needed. Imagine shopping for a cool, new, red sweater. You've done your research and you know the sweater costs

$40. You walk into your favorite store and discover the sweater is 25 percent off! Instead of spending $40, you pay $30. You walk out of the store with the sweater, and a $10 surplus in your pocket. Sweet!

The opposite situation occurs when you walk into the same store to find out the sweater you saw last week now costs $50. You decide to buy it anyway, and dip into some savings to do so. You've now created a $10 deficit.

The income-tax process provides another useful example of these concepts. If your employer has taken too much tax off your paychecks throughout the year, you'll probably end up getting a nice tax return in the mail (a surplus). If he or she hasn't taken enough, you'll end up owing money to the Internal Revenue Service (a deficit). The IRS Web sites is full of useful information to help you with the questions you may have about taxes. Check out www.irs.gov or call 1-800-829-1040. You can even download Publication 910 for information on free tax services provided by the IRS.

So how do you cope with these situations? Read on.

ASSETS AND LIABILITIES

Leave some room at the bottom of your budget spreadsheet to list your assets and liabilities. In financial terms, an asset refers to things you own (like a home, car, money, jewelry, bicycle, or even sports equipment). A liability generally refers to something you owe (tuition, a car loan, a mortgage, a debt). When you subtract your liabilities from your assets, you're left with your personal net worth—and there's nothing more exciting than watching it grow over time!

Under-Spending: A Surplus Is a Wonderful Thing

Let's start with the best-case scenario: your budget shows you have money left over at the end of each month. Congratulations! What are you going to do? Rush out and treat your ten closest friends to a night on the town? You might be able to afford it, but it wouldn't be the best plan in the long run.

Before visions of extra lattes and thousands of downloads start dancing through your head, think back to chapter 1 and your list of goals. What did you write down on page 26? You're now in the enviable position of having some extra cash to help make those dreams a reality. When we get to chapter 5, we'll talk specifically about how to save for items you want to buy in the short term. For now, simply remember you should always put aside money when you can afford to do so. Here are a few tips to help get you started:

IT'S OKAY TO REWARD YOURSELF

We've talked a lot about reining in your spending so you don't cause yourself financial grief. But it's also important to take pride in your income-earning ability, and reward yourself. Sometimes those rewards come through spending your money on things that are important to you. For example, every year I try to reward myself with a vacation. I take great pleasure in a few weeks off, exploring, relaxing, and having fun.

Tips for Dealing with a Surplus

If you're in the fortunate position of having a surplus, here are a few suggestions for what you might do with the extra cash:

- Open a savings account and start saving.
- Start an automated savings plan so you're saving and/or investing on a regular basis.
- Pay down high-interest debts (see chapter 4).
- Start a college fund.
- Contribute to a down payment for your first home.
- Contribute to a retirement-savings account like a 401(k), 403(b), IRA, Roth IRA and SEP IRA (see chapter 8 for more details).
- Reward yourself with *part* of the surplus—not *all* of it.

Overspending: The Dangers of Deficits

So, you're over your monthly budget. You're spending more than you earn, which might explain why you always have to borrow bus fare from your parents! What should you do? What *can* you do? You have three options: reduce your spending, increase your income, or borrow money. Obviously, the last option isn't always a good one. Let's look at some tips addressing the other two.

Tips for Dealing with a Deficit

- **Question everything.** Look carefully at your budget. What are your biggest expenses? Are you spending more money on clothes each month than you need to? Is your car insurance through the roof? Ask yourself if there are lifestyle changes you can make to reduce your monthly output of cash. Eliminating two pizza dinners each month, for example, could free up $35!

- **Look for opportunities.** Do you have the ability to increase your income? Can you take on a few more hours at work, or make a deal with your parents to do an additional household chore in exchange for an increase in your allowance? Are you driving friends to school every day? Might they be able to contribute a small amount to your gas costs? Do you have a hidden talent that could help you earn some money on the side? These things may seem insignificant, but every little bit helps.

- **Reorganize your priorities.** Put your savings and investing goals at the very top of your list of expenses. These should be nonnegotiable—more important to you than a few extra cable channels or an extra night out. Always pay yourself first—even if it's only $25 a month.

- **Examine your cash flow.** As much as we'd like them to be carved in stone, our expenses change from month to month. This affects your cash flow—a term used to describe the changes occurring in your expenses and income from month to month. You need to be aware of these fluctuations to have a firm grasp of your spending habits. For example, people tend to spend more in December because of the holidays. If you don't budget for this, you might end up with a big credit card bill near the end of January. The opposite situation can occur, as well. Are you taking a two-week holiday from work in the summer?

Remember to include your transportation costs in your budget for that month. The more aware you are of these fluctuations, the better able you'll be to handle them.

- **Plan for emergencies.** While you're revamping your budget, it's not a bad idea to include an expense dedicated to building an emergency fund. If your car broke down tomorrow, would you have enough money to fix it? If you lost your job next week, how would you cover your expenses until you found a new one? No one likes to spend more than they have, but things happen. Often, people don't plan for the unexpected. When an emergency occurs, they end up having to work overtime, pay high interest rates on a credit card, or do without something they really need. Some experts recommend you sock away the equivalent of six months' salary in your own emergency fund. That's a little excessive for the average person, so choose a number you find comfortable. Then, work it into your short-term savings plan (see chapter 5).

- **Avoid debt.** Only as an absolute last resort should you borrow money to cover your expenses. We'll talk lots more about debt in chapter 4, but for now, just realize that borrowing to pay for something you can't really afford is the first step down a very slippery slope. Before long, you'll be borrowing to pay off what you've already borrowed, and so on, and so on. It's much better to look at what you're buying, and ask yourself if you really need it. You'll be surprised at how often the answer is no.

Avoiding Home Poverty

When I graduated from university, I bought a townhouse. I was so excited about having a new job, a new home, living on my own—the whole package! Before too long, however, I ran right into an extremely common trap: home poverty. Basically, all I could afford was my house! I didn't have much money left over for anything else.

On paper, someone like me can make a healthy salary, but if I don't carefully monitor my cash flow, I could end up like many North Americans—bankrupt! Let's look at how this can happen, using Peter from our budget examples as a case study. Peter is twenty-five and works in the finance department of a local construction company. He recently bought a small condo and still has some student loans to pay off. Although he has a great job, he's still running out of money at the end of every month.

Let's look at his budget for November through to January to see how and why this is happening.

Peter in November

SOURCES OF INCOME	DOLLARS
Full-Time Job	2,800
Small Side Jobs	50
Total Monthly Income	**$2,850**

SOURCES OF EXPENSES	DOLLARS
Mortgage or Rent	850
Loan	300
Credit Card	125
Groceries	150
Investment Account	75
Heat	90
Property Tax	120

Electricity	55
Condo Fees	200
Home and Auto Insurance	125
Transit Tickets	70
Vehicle Fuel	120
Subtotal of Mandatory Expenses	**$2,280**
Bank Overdraft	0
Furniture Payment	100
Cell Phone Bill	65
Cable, Phone, Internet	125
Gym Membership	32
Subtotal of Secondary Expenses	**$322**
Fun Money	200
Subtotal of Fun Expenses	**$200**
Total Expenses	**$2,802**
Total Monthly Income	$2,850
Total Monthly Expenses	$2,802
Net Income or Loss	**$48**

As you can see, Peter is managing to juggle all of his payments, and he even has a little extra money for himself. In November, at least, he doesn't have an overdraft in his bank account. In December, however, things take a turn for the worse.

Peter in December

SOURCES OF INCOME	DOLLARS
Full-Time Job	2,800
Small Side Jobs	50
Total Monthly Income	**$2,850**
SOURCES OF EXPENSES	DOLLARS
Mortgage or Rent	850

Loan	300
Credit Card	125
Groceries	150
Investment Account	75
Heat	90
Property Tax	120
Electricity	55
Condo Fees	200
Home and Auto Insurance	125
Transit Tickets	70
Vehicle Fuel	120
Subtotal of Mandatory Expenses	**$2,280**
Bank Overdraft	0
Furniture Payment	100
Cell Phone Bill	65
Cable, Phone, Internet	125
Gym Membership	32
Subtotal of Secondary Expenses	**$322**
Holiday Gifts	500
Fun Money	200
Subtotal of Fun Expenses	**$700**
Total Expenses	**$3,302**
Total Monthly Income	$2,850
Total Monthly Expenses	$3,302
Net Income or Loss	**$(452)**

Ah, the holidays! You'll notice Peter spent a whopping $500 on holiday gifts in the month of December—a "fun expense" has turned his bottom line from a positive to a negative. It's too bad Peter didn't think ahead, and plan for this expense (after all, it's not like he didn't know the holidays were coming), because this seemingly small outlay of cash has a bit of a snowball effect. Check out what happens in January.

Peter in January

SOURCES OF INCOME	DOLLARS
Full-Time Job	2,800
Small Side Jobs	50
Total Monthly Income	**$2,850**
SOURCES OF EXPENSES	DOLLARS
Mortgage or Rent	850
Loan	300
Credit Card	125
Groceries	150
Investment Account	75
Heat	90
Property Tax	120
Electricity	55
Condo Fees	200
Home and Auto Insurance	125
Transit Tickets	70
Vehicle Fuel	120
Subtotal of Mandatory Expenses	**$2,280**
Bank Overdraft	452
Furniture Payment	100
Cell Phone Bill	65
Cable, Phone, Internet	125
Gym Membership	32
Subtotal of Secondary Expenses	**$774**
New Year's Sale Purchases	300
Fun Money	200

Subtotal of Fun Expenses	$500
Total Expenses	$3,554
Total Monthly Income	$2,850
Total Monthly Expenses	$3,554
Net Income or Loss	$(704)

Not surprisingly, Peter's net loss has increased. Why? Because he hasn't made any lifestyle changes to allow him to reduce his debt. Instead of curbing his shopping in January, for example, he goes out and takes advantage of the sales. Instead of using his fun money to pay down his debt from December, he spends it the same way he always does. If Peter continues to spend at this rate, his debt will continue to grow. And the worst part of all is even if he did stop his "extra" spending, his normal budget doesn't really allow him to start paying off the debt. It's quite likely Peter will end up carrying this debt for a long while—racking up interest charges along the way.

Scary, isn't it? Peter presents a perfect example of what can happen if you don't set realistic budgets, and stick to your cash-flow goals. As you can see, the amount of money "lost" increases every month. And he isn't making any real progress paying down the money he owes at the bank, either. He can't pay off his existing debt before a new pile plows him under each month. Debt builds on top of debt, thus creating more debt. If Peter continues in this vein, spending the same amount of money each month and not making any lifestyle changes, a bleak picture begins to emerge. He will borrow more and more money, dip into his savings, sell any assets he might have, and end up deeper and deeper in debt.

Surprisingly, many people find these "solutions" easier than making some obviously needed lifestyle changes. But changing the way you live is by far the most effective solution! Here are some ideas to help get you started, and there will be more information on living frugally in chapter 5:

- **Consider finding a roommate** with whom you can split the rent/mortgage, utilities, and grocery bills.
- **Follow recommended heating and electricity practices** to help reduce your monthly bills. For example, turn off your lights and computer before you head off for work. Also, ensure you have the proper weather stripping on all doors and windows.
- **Cut the cable.** As painful as this may seem, cable isn't a necessity. Grab a book or borrow some movies from the library.
- **Perform your own maintenance.** You'd be surprised how many people pay others to do things they could actually do themselves. Hey, if you feel entrepreneurial, you could make money doing other people's housecleaning, lawn maintenance, leaf raking, or snow shoveling.
- **Downsize.** eBay is a wonderful way to get rid of things you don't need—and gain a little extra income in the process.
- **Buy used.** If you need to replace something in your home, consider purchasing it used. Often, you can save hundreds if not thousands of dollars.

We've touched on debt just a bit in this chapter, but it really is a key concept. Before we talk more specifically about how to save and invest your hard-earned cash, let's spend a little more time trying to understand how not to get caught in the credit crunch.

4

Get Out from Under:

AVOIDING THE CREDIT CRUNCH

If there's one thing that can put the brakes on a good financial plan, it's a whopping pile of debt. Let's take a few minutes to examine the debt factor: why we're in it, how to pay it down if we are, and, perhaps most importantly, how to avoid it altogether!

The Money Pit

Money seriously doesn't grow on trees. As obvious as this may seem, our under-thirty generation spends it as if it does. In North America, since 1989, disposable income (the income left over after you've paid your taxes) has grown only 1.8 percent annually. Consumer spending, on the other hand, has grown at an annual rate of 2.6 percent. Clearly, we're spending way more than we earn—and racking up huge amounts of debt along the way. An American average household income in 2005 was just under $59,000 with that same household having more than $8,000 in credit card debt. Scary!

So what does all this mean in dollar figures? In North America, the youth market spends more than $112.5 billion each year, and we have a huge influence on household purchases. The average twelve- to thirteen-year-old has $1,500 to spend each year, while the average sixteen- to seventeen-year-old spends $4,500. Over the age of seventeen, figures vary greatly due to educational or career choices. Typically, young people have more spending money than their parents or guardians (who tend to pay out of their earnings for things like housing, heat, and electricity).

Because the youth market has relatively few financial obligations, we tend to spend our money on things we want, and rarely on things we need. Consider Anne, a typical sixteen-year-old still living at home. Her parents or guardians buy her clothes and food, and pay for her shelter. She may even be given an allowance for doing things around the house. With virtually none of her needs neglected, Anne has the opportunity to spend her money on whatever it is she wants. (On the opposite end of the spectrum, of course, a struggling young student may face an entirely different situation. His money may go toward groceries, rent, tuition, and books. Chances are his budget is very tight.)

But back to the average sixteen- or seventeen-year-old for a moment. If we take that $4,500 as an accurate figure, it breaks down to approximately $375 spending money each month. Where is all this cash going?

How We Get Sucked In

Keaton, seventeen, and Claire, sixteen, have been dating for about six months. On the weekends—when they aren't cramming in their homework—you can usually find them at the mall. They both love to shop for music, clothes, and whatever else they feel like buying! After a full day of power shopping, they often join their other friends for dinner and a movie. It isn't uncommon for each of them to spend $80 every weekend.

Like Keaton and Claire, many young people are spending the bulk of their money at the mall! We tend to visit the mall at least once a week, and spend an average of $46.80 each time. Add that up over the course of a year, and we're spending $2,433.60!

Why are we spending so much? There are some very powerful marketing and advertising forces out there! The amount of money spent on retail advertising has increased every year for decades. Between 2003 and 2004, for example, advertisers increased their budgets by 17 percent. No wonder we're compelled to shop! Advertising messages are extremely convincing, and they all say the same thing: "You *need* to have this service or product, and you need to have it *now*."

Essentially, our generation ends up trapped in debt because of so-called retail therapy. Swayed by all this advertising, we shop to make ourselves happy. We watch beer commercials and think if we drink that brand, we'll live that kind of life. We buy skin cream because we want to look like the model in the ad. We're chasing the dreams the advertising companies put out there for us, and we like doing it! We tend to be happy with our purchases—at least until the credit card bill arrives in the mail.

Although marketing and advertising forces are strong, you can turn the tables and use them to your advantage—as a source of knowledge rather than persuasion. When you're in the market for a vehicle, for example, do some research into what's out there. Use advertisements to find out more about the vehicle (price, safety, quality, etc.). You can then compare models and brands. With any medium and large product or service you want to purchase, it's a good idea to do some research and get the facts so you can make the best decision.

Shopping around can actually be fun. When I was in university, my friend Laura was in the market for a car. She had been driving around in a "beater" for years, and had finally saved enough to purchase a quality used car. Laura took a few months to make her decision about which vehicle to buy. She searched the Internet for quality and safety ratings. She spoke with friends who had vehicles she might be interested in. She test drove her "picks" a number of times. Slowly, she narrowed down her search to her two favorite cars. Then she began speaking with dealerships and private owners about price. She chose an Acura RSX and got an absolutely great deal. She saved money by not buying a brand new car. She saved money by taking the time to negotiate on the price. Lastly, because she did her research, she saved money by not getting ripped off. Laura is now a very happy car owner who didn't have to break the bank to get what she wanted.

Debt, Debt, and More Debt: The Dangers of Interest

So we've established that spending money is fun—we like to buy things we want and need! And it's clear most of us are pretty good at it, too! All we need to do is think of something we want, find it, purchase it, and voilà, the money is spent.

That's the happy side of the coin. The scary side is we often don't have the money needed to make the purchase, but we make the purchase anyway. How? We go into debt.

Because credit is so readily available, we've become very comfortable with the idea of owing money. Most of us have credit cards, and we don't hesitate to use them. We live in a buy-now-pay-later society, and we fully expect to get the things we crave without having to wait or save up. We throw the purchase on the credit card, and have to work extra hours so we can pay for our fancy new items. What's worse, these fancy new items end up costing us more than we should really be paying. If we can't pay the bill in full at the end of the month, the credit card company charges us interest, usually between 17 and 20 percent! Remarkably, many store credit cards charge even higher interest rates— some in the range of 28 or 29 percent. The nastiest part about the whole thing is that typically, credit card companies compound their interest charges daily—not monthly. Now, the happy feeling we got from instant gratification has forced us into a situation where we're continually paying for the past, rather than investing in the future! Doesn't feel so good anymore, does it?

Let's take a minute to really look at this phenomenon. Let's say you purchase a few new outfits from your favorite store at a cost of $600. Let's also say you pay for them with your regular credit card, which charges you 19.5 percent. The minimum payment on the bills you receive is likely about 3 percent of your total balance, meaning 3 percent of $600 is $18 (depending on your interest rate, the card, and the credit agreement—most credit cards will have a minimum payment set between 2 and 6 percent of the balance owed or $10—whichever is the higher value). Because of the way interest is calculated on credit cards (compounded daily), if you make only that minimum payment, you'll barely be covering the interest! Almost none of your payment will go toward the principal amount owing. If you were to stick to this approach—paying only the original minimum payment of $18 each month—it would take you approximately forty-nine months to pay off that initial $600. Even worse, the "true" cost of your borrowing (principal plus interest paid) would be just over $874!

If, however, you can pay off your balance within thirty days, you don't pay any interest at all. Before you whip out that card, think about whether you can afford to pay it off. If it's going to take you months to clear your balance, you might want to hold off on your purchase. Check out the credit/debt calculators on www.consumercredit.com or www.bankrate.com to find out what your credit card balance is *really* costing you!

WHEN IS A CREDIT CARD A GOOD THING?

Credit cards aren't *all* bad. They can be very useful in building your credit rating, which is also known as your FICO score. FICO stands for Fair Isaac Corporation, which is the name of the firm that created the formula for determining your three-digit credit score. The higher your FICO score, the more success you'll have getting better interest rates on loans, mortgages, credit cards, and the like. A lower score affects your ability to borrow money at good rates, get rental applications approved, and even sign up for things like cell phone plans. FICO scores range from 300 (not good) to 850 (very good), and they tend to be subdivided into ranges to help determine the interest rates you're charged on borrowed funds. You can check on your FICO score for free once a year with the three main credit bureaus: Equifax, Experian, and TransUnion. It's important to check this out, monitor it, and always try to make it better!

Your credit score impacts your life. To borrow money, you need proof you're responsible enough to pay it off. A credit card offers a good opportunity for you to show potential creditors you can indeed manage debt.

Credit cards also enable us to book vacations, shop online, pay tuition, and so on. And they can be very useful if you ever run into trouble. For example, my car broke down one summer about three hundred miles from home. I used my credit card to pay the mechanic. I made it home safely, and paid off my bill with my next paycheck.

Digging Your Way Out

Mike is a twenty-four-year-old electrician's apprentice. When he was between eighteen and nineteen years old, he managed to rack up about $21,200 in debt. He got himself into a lot of financial trouble making it very difficult for him to borrow at good interest rates. He is still paying off his debt.

Does Mike's situation sound familiar to you? Have you gotten yourself in over your head? Are you looking at a pile of credit card bills, with no idea of how to pay them off? First, I'd suggest you go back and reread the sections on living the frugal life. Trust me, it will help. The basic idea, though, is this: you need to reduce your expenses to free up some cash. Once you free up the cash, you can start paying down the debt. (Oh, and cut up that card before you get yourself into any more trouble!)

The debt-reduction strategy we're going to work through over the next few pages is designed for individuals who are really squeezed for cash. It's also dead simple. Get ready. A debt-free future is within reach.

STEP 1: Find a Roll of Wrapping Paper. Yup, wrapping paper. Get your hands on some old, forgotten roll that's lurking in the back of a closet. Roll out a two to three foot section, and tape it to your wall (colored side in!).

STEP 2: Identify Your Debts. Now, take a pen and write down all your debts—credit cards, loans, the $10 your buddy lent you last week. Then, below each item, note the interest rate, starting balance, and minimum payment due. Let's use Mike, from above, as a working example. His table is below. Yours will end up looking similar.

	VISA	AMERICAN EXPRESS	CAR LOAN	STUDENT DEBT
Interest Rate (%)	19.50	18.50	9.50	5.90
Starting Balance	$1,200	$1,000	$9,000	$10,000
Minimum Payment	$65	$35	$150	$200

As you put this table together, pay particular attention to the interest-rate row. If you're like most people who find themselves in debt, you're more focused on the amount owing than on the interest rate. This is a common mistake. It may be more gratifying to pay off the smaller debts first, but if you're paying more interest on the larger debts, it's wise to turn your attention to those at the outset (more on this in Step 4, below).

STEP 3: Make Debt Reduction Part of Your Budget. Now the fun part starts. Every month, you need to make sure you're in a position to make at least your monthly payments. To do this, you must place these minimum payments at the very top of your monthly budget (that is, after you pay yourself first). In Mike's case, he's looking at a total debt reduction expense of $450 per month ($65 + $35 + $150 + $200). So, go ahead and make those payments. Put an X below any debt you've made your regular payment on.

STEP 4: Make Use of Your Spare Change. Next, you need to turn your attention to the debt with the highest interest rate. Each month, do your absolute best to put a little extra toward this debt—even as little as $20 will help. In Mike's example, he'd want to put his extra cash toward his VISA bill. The interest rate, at 19.5 percent, is the highest of the bunch. A great trick to learn about extra payments is to space them so they're made approximately two weeks after your first payment. Because of the way interest rates are calculated (especially credit cards), you can significantly reduce the amount of time it takes to pay off your debt.

STEP 5: One Down, Three to Go. Once you've paid off the highest-interest-bearing debt, you can pat yourself on the back and move on to the next-highest-interest charger! For Mike, it's American Express. He'd go back to Step 3 and do the whole thing over again, making the minimum payment on everything and throwing any extra money onto his American Express card two weeks after the minimum payment. This time, however, finding that little bit of extra cash shouldn't be as hard—after all, Mike's just freed himself from having to pay VISA every month. In fact, he has an extra $65 to spend these days. Once he pays off the American Express, he can go back and narrow it down even further.

That's it! It's really that simple. The chart on pages 73 and 74 is a condensed version of a chart spanning five years, showing two payments each month. This is just one theoretical example of how this method of debt reduction can work. It might take more or less time for you, depending on your unique situation and the way that your financial institution charges interest on borrowed funds. Your minimum payments may also be different. The great thing about this chart, however, is you can adapt it to suit your needs.

Ultimately, the best solution to debt reduction is to not get into debt in the first place. Or, avoid accumulating more debt while you're reducing your old debt. If you can avoid debt, you'll end up having more available cash flow. More cash for you means more options. The more options and choices you have, the more freedom you have. Keep in mind it's super easy to spend $1,000. I could do it in thirty minutes. But it's much harder to pay it back!

Condensed Payment Plan

	VISA CARD	AMERICAN EXPRESS CREDIT CARD	CAR LOAN	STUDENT LINE OF CREDIT
Interest Rate	19.50%	18.50%	9.50%	5.90%
Starting Balance	$1,200.00	$1,000.00	$9,000.00	$10,000.00
Minimum Payment	$65.00	$35.00	$150.00	$200.00
1-Jun-06	X	X	X	X
15-Jun-06	$30	N/A	N/A	N/A
1-Jul-06	X	X	X	X
15-Jul-06	$30	N/A	N/A	N/A
1-Aug-06	X	X	X	X
15-Aug-06	$30	N/A	N/A	N/A
...				
...				
...				
1-Jun-07	X	X	X	X
15-Jun-07	$30	N/A	N/A	N/A
1-Jul-07	X	X	X	X
15-Jul-07	$30	N/A	N/A	N/A
1-Aug-07	GONE	X	X	X
15-Aug-07	GONE	$65	N/A	N/A
...				
...				
...				
1-Jun-08	GONE	GONE	X	X
15-Jun-08	GONE	GONE	$100	N/A
1-Jul-08	GONE	GONE	X	X
15-Jul-08	GONE	GONE	$100	N/A
1-Aug-08	GONE	GONE	X	X
15-Aug-08	GONE	GONE	$100	N/A

	VISA CARD	AMERICAN EXPRESS CREDIT CARD	CAR LOAN	STUDENT LINE OF CREDIT
...				
...				
...				
1-Jun-09	GONE	GONE	X	X
15-Jun-09	GONE	GONE	$100	N/A
1-Jul-09	GONE	GONE	X	X
15-Jul-09	GONE	GONE	$100	N/A
1-Aug-09	GONE	GONE	X	X
15-Aug-09	GONE	GONE	$100	N/A
1-Jun-10	GONE	GONE	GONE	X
15-Jun-10	GONE	GONE	GONE	$225
1-Jul-10	GONE	GONE	GONE	X
15-Jul-10	GONE	GONE	GONE	$225
1-Aug-10	GONE	GONE	GONE	X
15-Aug-10	GONE	GONE	GONE	$225
1-Oct-10	GONE	GONE	GONE	GONE

X = Regular Payment

N/A = No Extra Payments

... = Time Passes (Until Debt is Eliminated)

CONSOLIDATION

If your debt situation is really, really bad, you might want to consider a consolidation loan. A consolidation loan is where all your debts are wrapped into one loan at a lower interest rate, allowing you to make one monthly payment instead of three or four or more. I highly recommend talking to your financial adviser about whether you could qualify. They're sometimes difficult to get, but if you don't ask, you'll never know.

Sometimes debt can spiral way out of control, in which case, you may need credit counseling. In this situation, you work closely with a credit counselor who can help you develop a plan to beat your debt and negotiate with creditors. They also give solid advice aimed at helping you avoid bankruptcy. If you're sliding down the slippery slope of debt faster than you can dig your way out, contact a credit counseling agency, like the Association of Independent Consumer Credit Counseling Agencies (www.aiccca.org), National Foundation for Credit Counseling (www.nfcc.org) or Consumer Credit Counseling Services (www.cccsintl.org).

The key with a consolidation loan is to not get into any additional debt while you're making payments. You don't want to take three years to pay off your loan, then have to get another one because you haven't been responsible with your money.

A Little More Information on Biweekly Payments

We talked briefly about this above, but the biweekly payment plan is worth spending a little more time on—especially if you're dealing with a large debt.

Reducing your debt with biweekly payments, also known as an accelerated biweekly payment plan, allows you to put more of your coin on the principal amount owing, rather than on the accrued interest. By doing so, you end up reducing your debt faster than you would if you made one combined principal-plus-interest payment each month.

Let's say that you're carrying a $40,000 balance on your credit card (extreme, I know, but it will help make a point). On that amount of debt, your minimum monthly payment would be at least $800 or 2 percent of your balance owing (again, depending on your interest rate, the card, and the credit agreement—most credit cards will have a minimum payment set between 2 and 6 percent of the balance owed or $10—whichever is the higher value). In the initial stages of your payments, with an interest rate of 19.5 percent, approximately $650 of that payment would be applied to interest penalties and only $150 to the principal debt. As time passes and if you carry on paying $800 each month, more of your payment goes towards the principal and less towards interest expenses. At this rate, you'd be looking at just under nine years' worth of payments before you were debt free! The primary reason it is so expensive to carry a balance is because credit card companies take the interest rate you pay, divide it by 365 days and compound it *each day!*

For argument's sake, let's say that you paid $1,000 a month each month for the first year on that $40,000 credit card balance. By the end of the twelve-month period, your remaining balance would be just under $35,500. A little depressing, considering that you've put $12,000 onto your credit card! If you continue these monthly payments, it will take you approximately five and a half years to pay off that original balance.

Now let's look at what happens if you pay $500 every two weeks instead. By the end of the twelve-month period—after twenty-six payments—your remaining balance would be just under $34,300. If you continue these biweekly payments, it will take you approximately 4.8 years to pay off that original balance.

If you follow this to its natural conclusion, with biweekly payments all the way through, you'll save over $4,000 when we compare total principal and interest paid. And you'll save time as well.

By the way, a biweekly payment is also very beneficial with other large debts, like mortgages and car payments because it allows you to accelerate the payment process. For argument's sake, let's say you currently pay $1,000 per month as a mortgage payment. If you paid half the regular monthly payment, $500 every two weeks (biweekly), you end up paying $13,000 every year versus $12,000 in payments. This is because there are 26 biweekly payments (52 weeks divided by 2-week intervals) of $500 each. Again, the reason why biweekly payments are so popular is you end up reducing the amount of time it takes to pay down that debt because you're chipping away at more principal, the original big amount, and therefore you save money on interest costs. In addition to this, many Americans are paid biweekly, so they can align their payments with their paychecks.

Now, paying an extra $1,000 every year means on a monthly basis you end up having to produce an extra $83.33 ($1,000 divided by 12 monthly payments), and biweekly means producing an extra $38.46 ($1,000 divided by 26 biweekly payments). Overall, for most Americans, the increase in the payment tends to be an insignificant amount of money, sometimes an additional $15 to $50 per payment. The great thing about this insignificant increase is that it has a significant impact on the amount of time it takes you to pay off your debt. For example, if you purchase a home with a thirty-year mortgage, a biweekly payment will reduce your amortization period (the amount of time you'll be paying off the loan!). For instance, let's say your monthly payment is $1,000 and you switch to an accelerated biweekly payment of half the regular monthly amount. If your interest rate is in the range of 6 percent, you'll reduce your amortization period by about five years. So rather than taking thirty years to pay it off, you're looking at less than twenty-five. Neat trick!

In the example above, it's important to note that biweekly payments don't always work for everyone. First off, when you want to pay biweekly on a mortgage, it can cost $250 to $500 to set up, plus about $3 per transaction. I still think it's worth the initial start-up costs, because you save money you would have paid in interest through the extended length of your mortgage. Also, if your money is really tight, as in you've budgeted down to the last $15 or $50, it might not be possible to take advantage of this trick. I'd recommend, as your financial situation improves over time (*Rich by Thirty* will play a key role in this) and you start making more money, switch to a biweekly payment to take advantage of the opportunity of reducing the amount of time it takes you to pay off your loan.

So what's the bottom line? The best way to avoid debt is to start living the frugal life, and focus on saving for your future. By making your savings a priority, you'll be motivated enough to overcome the temptations of debt. Remember, you are saving for your financial well-being— for your own goals and dreams. In the next chapter, we're going to get specific about how to do just that.

5

Get Saving:

RIGHT HERE, RIGHT NOW

Saving money is different from investing money. You save money for things you want in the short term—things like a vacation, new computer, bicycle, or a down payment on a home or vehicle. Investing is for the long term. Think retirement.

If you're diligent about saving, you can indeed have the things you want. And because of the short time frame, it's actually a pretty rewarding process. For example, throughout university, I saved money toward a very small down payment on a home. When I graduated, all my scrimping and saving paid off when I got to enjoy my new townhouse. Investing is also rewarding, but it is harder to see your end goal if your time horizon is forty years down the road.

So, let's think about saving as something you do for things you'd like to achieve within one to three years. You might, for example, save for a vacation over the course of two years by depositing money into your savings account every time you get paid. You'll only earn a little bit of interest this way, but there's no risk involved. The money you put in will be there when you're ready to take it out.

Saving 101

Eighteen-year-old Rebecca is getting ready to head off to university in the fall. She has been attempting to save her money so she can buy a new laptop for her studies. After a few months of trying, she has given up! She just can't seem to make progress. Now, school is just two months away, and if she's going to get a laptop, she's going to have to borrow some coin to do so.

Does Rebecca's story sound familiar? Do you have any idea what she's doing wrong? If you've read chapter 2, you know she's not approaching her goals in an organized way. She doesn't have a plan for action, and that's bound to lead to disappointment. To save successfully, you need to have a clear sense of your goals, and a plan for getting there.

Like investing, which we'll discuss in chapters 6 and 7, saving requires some dedication. With so many tempting products on the market these days, it's difficult to save! You could easily blow through $1,000 at the mall in two hours—but it could take a full year to put that money back into your savings account. Yes, it's challenging not to give in to temptations, but the end result will be great. Down the road, you'll have more money than most people your age. And that money will help you make your dreams realities.

Making It Work: The Frugal Life

Meet Aaliyah. She's a twenty-one-year-old university student who works part time as a server at a restaurant. Luckily, her job pays well. She can cover her tuition fees, and still save a little each month. To do this, however, she has to live a pretty frugal life. She packs a lunch, and only buys coffee once or twice a week. She borrows books, movies, and magazines from the library rather than buying them. She hits up the second-hand stores for her clothing. All of this is worth it, though. When Aaliyah is finished her degree, she'll have saved about $4,000—enough to take a trip or make a down payment, so she can start living on her own!

The key to being smart with your money is to live the frugal life. Now don't panic! This doesn't mean you have to penny pinch with absolutely everything. But it does mean you must be conscious of what you're spending and—more importantly—why. If you want to get a handle on your money, get a handle on your spending!

FRUGAL FUNDAMENTALS "Spend your money wisely." How many times have you heard that phrase? Was the person saying it a generation or two older than you? Don't let that fact change your opinion. Despite what you may want to believe, the phrase does have a lot of value. My friend Erin is the queen of frugal living. Over the years, she has given some great advice on being frugal (even to me), and some great tips on saving money. Together, we've developed a list of tips and tricks to help you live the frugal life:

- **Be Ruthless.** Before you plunk down your hard-earned cash, ask yourself whether you really *need* the item in question, or if you just *want* it. If you don't need yet another pair of strappy sandals, or a new set of speakers for your stereo, then you might want to reconsider its priority on your shopping list. Having trouble sorting it out? Try waiting twenty-four hours before buying. Often, you'll change your mind.

- **Cut the credit.** If your credit card is getting you into trouble, hide it! Get it out of your wallet. Give it to a parent or trusted adult to hold, or stick it in a resealable bag, fill the bag with water, and put the whole package in the freezer. By the time your cards have thawed, you'll have had a chance to think twice about making that "must have" purchase—and don't bother trying to hammer the ice; that will just wreck the cards.

- **Wheel and deal.** Everything is negotiable. If you feel your credit-card interest rate is too high, call and talk about it with a customer service representative. Negotiate better rates on your debt, on your cell phone bill, on your Internet service. Remember, if you don't ask, you don't get.

- **Pare down.** While you're in that wheeling-and-dealing mode, why not take a closer look at your various plans? Do you really need all those cable channels, or that many hours of Internet access each month? Do you need text messaging and voice mail on your cell phone? Think hard, and get rid of anything you don't need.

- **Become a bargain hunter.** Look for sales and discounts when you shop. Check out eBay, auctions, garage sales, and estate sales. I've done it and had great success. My dining-room table cost $50, my TV stand was $8, my stove was $60, and my two beautiful leather couches cost a total of $500! My grand total was $618. Had I purchased these items new, I would have paid nearly $3,500. You can also check out vintage stores for cool clothes, jewelry, and accessories.

- **Entertain yourself on the cheap.** Don't forget to apply the bargain-hunter rules to other areas of your life. If you enjoy going out for dinner and to the movies, keep your eyes open for coupons or two-for-one nights, or get to know the discount theatres in your neighborhood. Better yet, why not host a potluck and video night for your friends? Did you know most public libraries have a great collection of videos and DVDs? Yes, renting is cheaper than going to the movie theatre, but borrowing is free! (Hint: they loan CDs as well!)

- **Think about your food habits.** We spend a ton of money on food, whether we live with our parents or on our own. Here are a few ideas for everyone to keep in mind:

  - If you live at home, eat at home—or pack a lunch! Fast food is a budget killer and can add up to over $100,000 throughout your lifetime.

  - Stop drinking soda. You'll have more money and you'll be healthier.

  - Try cutting back on meat (vegetarian dishes are often cheaper to prepare).

  - Buy your food in bulk (the more you buy, the cheaper it gets).

  - And finally, trade in your "designer" coffee for a less expensive cup! (Better yet, buy a travel mug and bring your own hot beverage wherever you're going.)

- **Get healthy.** A healthy lifestyle can be remarkably affordable. Just think about it: if you drink or smoke, cutting down can put dollars back into your pocket and add years to your life. Walking or biking, instead of driving or taking public transit, will leave you feeling fit both physically and financially. Why not give it a try for a week and see what a difference it makes?

COMMIT YOURSELF!

Many successful financial advisers suggest saving at least 10 percent of everything you earn.

I think it's possible to save even more. If you're working and living on your own, why not aim for 20 percent? (I've been sticking to this goal for more than ten years now.) If you're living at home and are without expenses, such as a mortgage or rent, I challenge you to save 50 percent. You'll never have another opportunity to save this much again. Think about what you save each month. Commit to something realistic and write it in below:

I, _____, **commit to saving** _____
every month or every paycheck.

It's important to put your savings commitment above all your other financial commitments. Pay yourself first, because no one else will!

Simple, right? Sort of. It's not easy to change your lifestyle, or to cut back on things you really like, but it's worth it in the end. Think about it this way: If you were to cut out one fancy $3 coffee each weekday (you could treat yourself on weekends, if you absolutely had to!), you'd free up approximately $60 a month! That's $60 you could put toward your savings—for those shoes, that vacation, or a new car. It's your choice.

So, now that you've actually figured out how to free up some money, what do you do with it? Keep reading.

Making It Work

Meet Christopher, seventeen. His best friends are planning a ski trip to Whistler, BC, in twelve months. Christopher's parents have said he can go, if—and only if—he pays for the trip himself. With just one year to save, Christopher is a little nervous! He doesn't even know where to start.

With money, as with almost anything, the trick is to break things down to the basics. Christopher has one year to save $1,000. If you look at the year in terms of months, this means Christopher has to tuck away about $83 per month. Because he lives at home with his parents, and has very few expenses, saving that amount each month seems pretty reasonable. However, as we've already learned, saving money can be difficult. What if his car dies, or the speakers he really wants go on sale?

One way to ensure you don't get distracted from your savings goals is to commit yourself to a plan. By following a few easy steps, you'll be able to stick to that plan and achieve your savings goals.

- **Step 1: Write down Your Goals.** As we learned in chapter 1, it's much easier to stick to a plan if it's written down somewhere. In Christopher's case, he'd simply write, "I want to save $1,000 for a ski vacation in one year's time."

- **Step 2: Do the Math.** Once you know what you want, and when you want it, you can do more specific number crunching. For example, if Christopher needs to save $1,000 over one year, he should put away $83.33 a month for the next twelve months ($1,000/12 months = $83.33 per month).

- **Step 3: Open a Savings Account.** If you don't already have one, open a savings account that has a reasonable rate of return (they tend to vary from about 0.05 to 4 or 5 percent). When you speak to the bank representative, make sure the account is set up as "deposit only." This will ensure you cannot take money out of the account with your debit/ATM card. (When you've reached your savings goal, you can remove this designation, and allow yourself to access the money.)

- **Step 4: Automate Your Monthly Savings Contribution.** Have your financial institution automatically take your savings money from your checking account on the day you get paid. This automates your deposit so you don't have to do it yourself. You won't forget, and you won't be tempted to spend your money elsewhere. Most importantly, you'll be paying yourself first. In the box on page 84, I mentioned how important this is. You should be the number one financial priority in your life...not your creditors. If you don't put aside your savings and investing funds first, no one else will.

Christopher did manage to save his $1,000 in twelve months. He followed the steps outlined above and got his savings in gear. Christopher also lived pretty frugally! He saved about $30 a week by not buying lunch every day (he allowed himself a lunch out once a week, as a treat). He put those savings toward his ski trip and even had a bit of money left over. Because he worked so hard to save his money, Christopher thoroughly enjoyed himself. He earned it!

GET AUTOMATED!

Automated banking services are handy for all sorts of reasons. Every time I get paid, my employer deposits money into my bank account. On that same day, my savings and investing money is electronically transferred from my checking account into the next appropriate account. I also have my bills set up to be paid electronically on the day they're due. This lets me keep my money in my bank account until I have to make a payment. I'm gaining interest on that amount, while I wait for the due date. These electronic transfers don't take much of my time at all, because I set them up ahead of time. The only thing I do is check up on my financial situation for about ten minutes every week. Most of the major financial institutions have online bill-payment options. If you don't deal with an institution that does, you can still pay bills online using services like www.quickenbill-pay.com or www.finance.yahoo.com/bp.

What Are You Saving For?

When you imagine yourself one to three years down the road, what tangible things do you see? Do you own a particular vehicle, or live in a certain community? Perhaps you see yourself pursuing your education. Write down some of your visions for the not-too-distant future. In particular, identify some of the things for which you'd like to save.

_____

_____

_____

_____

_____

Now, go back and pencil in a price beside each item you wrote down. You may have to look on the Internet or grab a newspaper to make sure you're being realistic about this.

Got it? Okay. Let's just say the first item on your list is a car, and let's say you're being pretty honest about the whole thing. You know the newest BMW isn't likely to be sitting in your driveway three years from now, so you're going to focus on something older, maybe even a little run-down. Something you can use to get from point A to point B. Nothing fancy, just practical. Let's say you're budgeting $6,000 for this used car.

But there's also item number two. Let's say your family computer is ancient, and you know you're going to need a new one to keep up with your school work. Unlike the car, which can wait a while, you'd really like that computer in two years. And you figure it's going to cost you $2,000.

So, you know what you want. Let's do some math, and figure out what it's going to take to get it for you. The key thing is to figure out how much you're going to need to save each month. You do this according to a monthly savings formula, which looks like this:

purchase price/number of months until purchase date = monthly savings

For the computer, the formula goes like this:

$2,000/24 months = $83.33 per month

And for the car:

$6,000/36 months = $166.67 per month

To purchase both things, you'd need to save $250 a month ($83.33 + $166.67) for the next twenty-four months. At that point, you could buy your computer and continue saving $166.67 a month for the next twelve months. At the end of that period, you'd have enough for your car as well.

How much will you have to save each month so you can have some of the bigger things you want? You can try this calculation with the savings items you have listed above. Just take the purchase price and divide it by the number of months within which you want to have that item. Your result will tell you how much money you need to save every month to make your goal a reality.

Item 1: _____

_____ (purchase price)/_____ (months) = _____ (savings per month)

Item 2: _____

_____ (purchase price)/_____ (months) = _____ (savings per month)

Item 3: _____

_____ (purchase price)/_____ (months) = _____ (savings per month)

How did you do? Sometimes, we find the items we want cost more than we thought—or it will take us much longer to save for them than we imagined. If you found your monthly savings amount was too high for your budget, try extending the amount of time it takes to save by increasing the number of months you put into your calculation. On the flip side, perhaps you've found your monthly savings amount was less than you expected! If that's the case, you might be able to save more every month and so, you can shorten your time horizon by reducing the amount of months you put into your calculation.

One of the most rewarding experiences you can have is spending your hard-earned savings on your own goals. Enjoy it, and enjoy your rewards!

Bumps in the Road

Pedro has been working a part-time job since he was sixteen. He is now twenty and has been saving his money at a rate of $150 per month for the past four years. He now has about $7,200 to put toward a vehicle. However, when an overseas relative passed away, he needed to attend the funeral. He had no choice but to dip into his savings account for a plane ticket, a new suit, accommodations, flowers and meals. Now, he's down about $3,000, and he's pretty much given up on his dreams of owning a vehicle for another two years.

Life brings about some unexpected changes—changes that can affect both your ability and motivation to save. However, when it comes to your financial health, you have to roll with the punches and carry on. If you don't, you aren't going to achieve your goals. Here are a few things you can do when the unexpected happens:

- **Recognize when your plans are getting off track.** The only way you'll be able to do this is to be organized with your money. Use tools like online banking to keep track of where money is going and why. You might be able to recognize a nasty trend before it depletes your entire savings.
- **Never give up.** Even when you're discouraged, don't give up on your financial dreams. You'll never achieve them if you do.
- **Get back into your healthy financial habits.** If you've been forced to veer from a savings plan, start it up again as soon as you're able. Don't let a temporary twist in the road become permanent.

- **Be proactive, not reactive.** Try to predict, as best you can, what events will impact your finances and plan for them in advance. For example, if you know you have to pay for tuition in a year, brace yourself for the expense.

EMERGENCY FUNDS

When you start to get organized with your money, I highly recommend setting up a little emergency fund—and make sure you only use it for emergencies! Ensure you have enough cash to carry you through things like loss of employment, vet bills, car repairs, etc. You're the only one who can determine what amount of money you should set aside every month. I take about 5 percent of my net pay and throw it into my savings account as an emergency fund. I've found that number works well for me. But consider your situation and how much money you'll need, if and when an emergency arises.

An emergency fund should be built along with your savings and investing. One of the keys to successful finances is balance. Balance your spending, saving and investing, emergency funds, and debt reduction.

6
Get Investing, Part I:
THE BASICS

So, you have the motivation, the goals, and some basic financial fundamentals under your belt. You know how to properly budget and you've identified areas in your budget where you might free up some dollars. Now it's time to get down to the nitty gritty of investing. In this chapter, we're going to cover some investment basics—why to invest, what type of investor you are, what all those strange terms mean. In chapter 7, we'll look specifically at the various investment options and strategies. Hang in for the ride, because this information is valuable. It's your ticket to becoming a millionaire.

Why Should I Invest?

What comes to mind when you hear the word "investing"? The most common response invariably has to do with money. For many of us, investing refers to the actions we take when we put money into the marketplace, a home, a stock, or a bond. But if we broaden our scope a little, we realize the term can be used to describe many other things. You can invest in your education, for example, or invest your time. At its most basic, investing means you're building your resources—whatever those may be.

You're an investor right now! You're investing in your education by reading this book. You're also investing your time and energy. And, as with any good investment, your efforts will pay off with increased financial knowledge and better financial health.

Just as investing means different things to different people, people chose to invest for their own personal reasons. I want to invest my money for the future. I also want to invest it for the present. When I think of investing any of my money, I have five primary objectives:

1) **Safety:** I want to invest my money in a way that ensures I won't lose it all.
2) **Income:** I want to use my invested money as income in the future.
3) **Growth:** I want to grow my money using the power of compound interest.
4) **Liquidity:** I want to invest my money in things that are easy to buy and sell.
5) **Tax Minimization:** I want my investments to help minimize the taxes I pay.

If you're scratching your head and wondering what the heck I'm talking about, don't worry. You're about to learn that good investments can meet all of these objectives. For now, I just want you to think about your investment goals. What do you want to achieve?

If you're still scratching your head, try flipping back to chapter 1. In the chart on page 27, you wrote down some of your personal and financial goals. What were your long-term goals? Where do you want to be ten, twenty, or fifty years from now? Do you want to retire at forty-five, and sail your yacht around the world? Own a family cottage on the shores of a northern lake? When you're considering your future—specifically, anything more than three years away—you need to shift your financial thinking from short term to long term. And to achieve long-term financial success, you must invest your money.

Over the long haul, money grows much faster if it's invested rather than simply saved. Investment offers a greater potential for a higher return. History backs me up on this. For the past two hundred years, investments in things like stocks, bonds, and mutual funds have consistently outperformed the lowly savings account. Check out the chart below:

Power of Saving and Investing

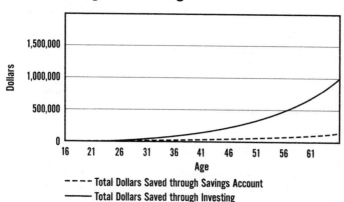

- - - - Total Dollars Saved through Savings Account
——— Total Dollars Saved through Investing

Saving your money is always better than spending it, but investing for the long term is the best idea of all.

The Power of Interest

So how does this work? Investing makes more money than savings over the long haul because of compound interest. We talked about this a bit back in chapter 1, when we were discussing the importance of time. Compound interest is like growing your money for free. You earn interest on your initial investment. That interest is reinvested, and you end up earning interest on it, as well. Now, you're earning interest on your interest. How cool is that?

The chart below demonstrates the power of compound interest. If you start investing your money at the age of sixteen, you'll be a millionaire by the time you're sixty-five—and it takes only $35 per month to start! A savings account, on the other hand, will leave you with approximately one-tenth of that million-dollar payout. (The chart below along with the one above assumes an average rate of return of 8.5 percent on the investment and 1 percent on the savings account. It also assumes you invest the total dollars saved at the end of the year, rather than in monthly installments. This is for ease of calculation.)

In constructing this chart, I made a few basic assumptions. First, I assumed the investor would increase the amount invested each month at certain life stages. By twenty-three, for example, it's reasonable to expect most young people will have a slightly greater earning potential. They're either nearing completion of post-secondary education or they've already started in their career. Perhaps they're in a job that pays more than it used to. Whatever the reason, by twenty-three, most young people can afford

AGE	$'S SAVED PER MONTH	$'S SAVED PER YEAR	TOTAL $'S SAVED	$'S SAVED WITH SAVINGS INTEREST (1%)	TOTAL $'S SAVED THROUGH INVESTING (8.5%)
16	35	420	420	424.20	455.70
17	35	420	840	852.64	950.13
18	35	420	1,260	1,285.37	1,486.60
19	35	420	1,680	1,722.42	2,068.66
20	35	420	2,100	2,163.85	2,700.19
21	35	420	2,520	2,609.68	3,385.41
22	35	420	2,940	3,059.98	4,128.87
23	150	1800	4,740	4,908.58	6,432.82
24	150	1,800	6,540	6,775.67	8,932.61
25	150	1,800	8,340	8,661.42	11,644.88
26	150	1,800	10,140	10,566.04	14,587.70
27	150	1,800	11,940	12,489.70	17,780.65
28	150	1,800	13,740	14,432.60	21,245.01
29	150	1,800	15,540	16,394.92	25,003.84
30	250	3,000	18,540	19,588.87	30,384.16
31	250	3,000	21,540	22,814.76	36,221.81
32	250	3,000	24,540	26,072.91	42,555.67
33	250	3,000	27,540	29,363.64	49,427.90
34	250	3,000	30,540	32,687.27	56,884.27
35	250	3,000	33,540	36,044.15	64,974.44
36	250	3,000	36,540	39,434.59	73,752.26
37	250	3,000	39,540	42,858.93	83,276.21
38	250	3,000	42,540	46,317.52	93,609.68
39	250	3,000	45,540	49,810.70	104,821.51
40	350	4,200	49,740	54,550.80	118,288.33
41	350	4,200	53,940	59,338.31	132,899.84
42	350	4,200	58,140	64,173.70	148,753.33
43	350	4,200	62,340	69,057.43	165,954.36

AGE	$'S SAVED PER MONTH	$'S SAVED PER YEAR	TOTAL $'S SAVED	$'S SAVED WITH SAVINGS INTEREST (1%)	TOTAL $'S SAVED THROUGH INVESTING (8.5%)
44	350	4,200	66,540	73,990.01	184,617.48
45	350	4,200	70,740	78,971.91	204,866.97
46				79,761.63	222,280.66
47				80,559.24	241,174.52
48				81,364.83	261,674.35
49				82,178.48	283,916.67
50				83,000.27	308,049.59
51				83,830.27	334,233.80
52				84,668.57	362,643.68
53				85,515.26	393,468.39
54				86,370.41	426,913.20
55				87,234.12	463,200.82
56				88,106.46	502,572.89
57				88,987.52	545,291.59
58				89,877.40	591,641.37
59				90,776.17	641,930.89
60				91,683.93	696,495.02
61				92,600.77	755,697.09
62				93,526.78	819,931.35
63				94,462.05	889,625.51
64				95,406.67	965,243.68
65				$96,360.73	$1,047,289.39

to increase their monthly contribution. Additional increases, for similar reasons, happen at thirty and forty. Theoretically, after the age of forty-five, you could stop investing your money and just sit on it until you retire. If you did this, you'd have approximately $1 million by the time you retired.

These are just assumptions, and they don't take into account the unique situations in which you might find yourself. Maybe you'll be in school until you're twenty-eight, or end up earning a lot of money working overseas at age twenty. Whatever your circumstances, the key is to save and invest your money regularly to take advantage of compound interest starting at a young age.

Stick It Out!

Sandra is thirty-five years old. Five years ago, she temporarily lost her job and stopped investing. She didn't have any extra income and, besides, her money wasn't growing as fast as she'd hoped it would, anyway. She cashed in her investments, bought a condo and a car and, now, she's kicking herself because she has zero investment money saved for her retirement. Her best friend, who kept her money invested, is watching it grow. Sandra, on the other hand, worries about the future.

Looking at the chart on pages 97–98, one thing becomes obvious. Unlike savings (which can take place over time periods ranging from a few months to a few years), investing is a long-term proposition. You need patience and commitment to stick to your plan. At the beginning, you may get discouraged by what seems to be a lack of progress (it takes a while for that compound interest thing to really kick in!). If you bail, like Sandra, you'll never achieve your financial goals. If you stick with it, however, you'll start to see the results as time passes, and motivation will no longer be a problem!

Can you think of any reasons why investing over the long term might be difficult for you? Are you an impulse shopper? Do you lack the funds needed to invest? Think about it for a moment, and then check out the following tips designed to help keep you on track:

- **Start as soon as possible.** The earlier you start, the more time you'll have to grow your money with compound interest and the sooner you'll see results. Also, investing every month will become a habit, making it easier to keep up as time passes.
- **Choose a reasonable amount of money to invest.** Strike a balance between the money you save and the money you invest. There's no point setting your goals too high; if you fail, you'll get discouraged and you might give up. When you create your own budget, think carefully about how much you can afford to set aside. And don't worry if the amount seems small. Even $10 a month is better than nothing!
- **Automate your monthly contribution.** Have your financial institution take your monthly investment contribution straight out of your bank account on the day you get paid. That way, you won't be tempted to spend your entire paycheck before you invest. Over time, you'll mentally adjust to not having this money. You won't even miss it!
- **Remind yourself you're doing well.** While you don't want to obsess over the financial details of your life,

it's not a bad idea to check on your accounts once a month to remind yourself you're making progress. Keep a chart on your wall, or set up a spreadsheet on your computer. Being able to visualize your success will help keep you on track.

Now that you're clear on why you should be investing, you can start to think about the types of investments that might work for you. In chapter 7, we'll look carefully at the various investment options available, but before you start throwing money at the hottest stock or trendiest mutual fund, there are a few more things you need to know—starting with yourself!

Investor, Know Thyself!

Would you feed your fish dog food? I doubt it. If you did, your fish (deprived of the nutrients it needs to survive) would likely end up floating at the top of its tank by the end of the week. Likewise, if you attempted to serve fish flakes to your dog, Fido wouldn't be a happy camper.

A young person's needs and desires are unique. Like the fish and the dog, each of us requires different things to satisfy our various needs. If these needs aren't met, we won't thrive. Our investment needs are no exception.

Unlike savings, which works in pretty much the same way for everyone, investing can be a highly personal undertaking. Before you dive in, it's a good idea to work up an investment plan. And before you can do that, you need to understand both your goals and your investment profile.

Investor Profiles

A happy investor is one whose investment goals and choices are properly aligned—someone who knows the types of investment options that will best suit his or her needs and personality. Discovering your investor profile isn't difficult. If you visit a bank with the intention of setting up an investment account, they'll likely present you with a long, drawn-out questionnaire, or ask you about a hundred questions—all designed to tell them what type of investment options would best suit your needs. Below are some of the most common questions. If you answer them honestly, you'll have a pretty good sense of your own investment profile.

WHAT ARE YOUR PERSONAL GOALS? Well! It's lucky we've already answered this one, isn't it? Refer back to chapter 1, and the discussion on goal setting. The goals you wrote down on page 27 will work just fine as an answer to this question.

WHAT IS YOUR INVESTMENT TIME HORIZON? This question is very important. Not all goals can be achieved with the same investment strategies. Take, for example, Rachel—a high-school student who is desperately trying to save for college. Let's say Rachel doesn't have access to student loans. Because she needs this money within a few years, and she can't afford to lose any of it, Rachel needs to put her money into a safe investment—one that won't lose value in the short term.

Someone with a longer investment time horizon, however, would have more time during which to make up losses and enjoy gains. This person's strategy would be very different from Rachel's.

WHERE WILL YOUR MONEY BE COMING FROM? Money from a regular income is different than money given to an individual on a one-time basis. This can affect the type of investment you choose. Kyle, for example, works on commission and gets paid every three months. If you're in a similar situation, your cash flow is going to be different from someone working a regular hourly wage job. Also, commission is temperamental, and can vary from time to time. Because Kyle's cash flow is all over the map, it's important for him to work out a reasonable investment plan that fits his money schedule.

DO YOU HAVE ANY TAX OR LEGAL CONCERNS? Many investors want to take advantage of tax considerations allowing them to pay less personal income tax. If this is one of your investment goals, there are a number of investments on the market to assist you.

WHAT ROLE DO YOU WANT TO PLAY WHEN IT COMES TO YOUR MONEY? Informing your investment adviser about how involved you want to be with your money will ensure they understand some of your needs. Your involvement will affect the choices you make and the workload your adviser has to do.

WHAT IS YOUR RISK TOLERANCE? This is the big one—the most important question of all, when it comes to determining your investment profile. Risk tolerance is a vital piece of the investment puzzle. To invest without going insane, you need to match your risk tolerance to your needs. If you don't like the idea of investments changing in value from day to day, you may not want to participate in the stock market. On the other hand, if you've got a stomach for handling the ups and downs of the market, you may want to take advantage of risky investments so you can benefit from a higher reward in the long run. You can have some fun with the following quiz to see what type of investor you are:

1) When your math teacher comes walking up to you with a grim "you're in trouble" look on her face you...
   a) listen as she accuses you of something you didn't do. You don't like confrontation, so you choose not to correct her.
   b) say, "I'm not exactly sure what the problem is. Can you explain what happened?" You then listen carefully to what she has to say.
   c) deny, deny, deny.

2) Some kids down the street received new cars for their birthdays. They want to race against your dad's new sports car—a car you're normally not allowed to go near. You...
   a) grab the keys to the shiny red roadster, and kick off the neighborhood Indy 500 in style.
   b) walk away from these bullies, without giving them an answer.
   c) tell them your dad's car is worth more than all theirs put together, and you'd rather eat dirt than face your father's wrath when he finds you with the keys in your hot little hands.

3) You're in a store where an attractive sales assistant works. She (or he) approaches you and asks if you need any help. You...

a) tell him/her you're looking for a pair of pants, and say you really like his/her outfit. Hey, if you find some equally trendy clothes, maybe he/she will ask for your number!

b) turn beet red and say, "Thanks, but I can find my own clothes."

c) say, "Sure, you can help me" and ask for his/her number when you're leaving.

4) You were given $1,000 for doing a great job at the local science fair. You would likely...

a) spend $400 on some new clothing, save $500 in your investment account, and donate $100 back to the science-fair committee.

b) take your closest friends out for a day of snowboarding and eating nachos. The cost of your trip would be $1,000.

c) stuff it all away under your mattress, or in your piggy bank.

5) You buy a new condo with your hard-earned money at the age of twenty-one. You've got a reasonable mortgage ($800 per month), a great interest rate, and a roommate who pays $400 each month in rent. You have an extra $300 a month after all your expenses, fun, and necessities are handled, so you...

a) pool your extra money with a friend, and buy another condo you could rent out.

b) pay down your existing mortgage as fast as possible (you don't like to be in debt).

c) use half the money to fix up your condo (adding value), and put the other half toward your mutual-fund investments.

Okay. Now tally your points according to the following:

1. a) 1 point   b) 2 points   c) 3 points
2. a) 3 points   b) 1 point   c) 2 points
3. a) 2 points   b) 1 point   c) 3 points
4. a) 2 points   b) 3 points   c) 1 points
5. a) 3 points   b) 1 point   c) 2 points

If you scored between 5 and 6 points, you're a low-risk investor. Your stomach will turn if you're forced into a situation outside your comfort zone. You probably aren't a huge risk taker. For example, you won't likely go cliff diving, or willingly give a speech in human-health class. Investing money in risky things that aren't guaranteed will not be part of your agenda. The benefit of being a low-risk investor is you'll be very careful when you choose your secure investment vehicles. When the markets get rocky, you won't lose much money. However, you won't make as much as your riskier counterparts in the long run.

If you scored between 7 and 11 points you're a moderate investor. The decisions you make aren't totally wild and off the wall. They tend to be carefully planned and considered. You might be willing to venture out of your comfort zone with your investment choices, but only if they won't endanger your long-term goals. Medium-risk investments are a great fit for you, because they earn a higher return than low-risk investments with only a slightly higher risk of loss. However, you're a person who can take loss fairly well. You wouldn't like it, but you'd pick up the pieces and make something new.

If you scored between 12 and 15 points, you're a high-risk investor and risky investment choices will suit your personality. You have the potential to make a lot of money when times are good, and to lose a lot of money when times are bad—if you don't protect yourself. If you're going to follow the high-risk-investor route, do so with a little caution. Include some safer choices in your mix as well, and remember, there are some investment options even professionals won't touch!

MAKING SENSE OF IT ALL

Grab a newspaper and turn to the financial section. Are your eyes glazing over yet? At first glance, it looks incredibly boring. But it isn't. The little tiny numbers written horizontally across the stock, bond, and mutual fund pages will always state the following information. The first column tells you the name of the investment. The next columns will have the volume traded the previous business day, the highest and lowest price throughout that day, the closing price, and the change from the previous day's price. Whatever newspaper you've chosen to examine, and whatever the order of information, there should be a legend or something to help you follow along. If you want things to start making sense, pick one stock from the stock market page and follow it daily for the next two weeks. You'll get the hang of it faster than you think!

An Investment Primer: Talking the Talk

You're almost there. You're almost ready to take the plunge. There's only one more thing you need to know. Okay...it's more than one thing. It's several things. Dozens maybe. As you read this chapter and the next, you're going to come across a lot of weird and wacky words you may not have seen before (you may have already encountered a few you don't fully understand). Before we start talking about bonds, Individual Retirement Accounts (IRAS), Certificates of Deposit (CDS), and the like (which will be defined in the next chapter), let's wrap our heads around some investing lingo:

- **Investment option or vehicle:** Anything (like a mutual fund, stock, bond, or treasury bill, to name a few) into which you can invest your money.
- **Investment portfolio:** Your personal combination of investment options. A portfolio is geared specifically to your needs and investment style. It can be high-risk, moderate-risk, low-risk, or somewhere in between.
- **Market:** A place where buyers and sellers meet to trade things of value. We buy and sell investments. Newspapers list the market prices for these items on those pages with all the tiny little numbers. There are two major stock markets in the United States: the New York Stock Exchange (NYSE), and the NASDAQ. There are also mutual-fund markets, money markets, bond markets, and more.

- **Market cycles:** Financial markets tend to experience cycles. Sometimes they perform well, sometimes poorly. This tends to happen in waves. When the markets are performing poorly, the economy is slow. The opposite is also true. The five most common market cycles are:
  - **Expansion:** An upward trend. New businesses and jobs are being created, and people are investing more money in the market. The economy is growing and inflation is stable. This is a good time to be purchasing investments, because they will grow in value throughout this cycle.
  - **Peak:** Labor shortages start, wages increase significantly, demand for product is high, and interest rates are very high. Because prices have increased significantly, the market begins to react negatively. Investments like stocks and bonds tend to be very expensive. This isn't a good time to be purchasing investments, homes, cars, or other big-ticket items. They're overpriced and can lose value in the next cycle.
  - **Recession or Contraction:** Economic activity begins to slow down. Unemployment rates start to rise, and there is less money available in the market. Typically, it is a difficult time for people to save or invest any money whatsoever.
  - **Trough:** The lowest part of the business cycle. Prices have fallen substantially, and so have interest rates. Consumers tend to be short on cash, but because of low interest rates, they're able to borrow money and purchase items like homes and investments at lower prices. This is the best

time to purchase investments, because they can be very undervalued.

- **Recovery:** An expansionary cycle during which the market starts to return to its previous peak. Many big-ticket items are purchased throughout this time and, because of the increase in demand, prices start to increase again. This is a good time to be purchasing investments, because the prices are still relatively low.

Markets change from year to year. Overall, however, the stock and mutual fund markets in North America have survived the ups and downs, and provided an average return between 10 percent and 12 percent when looking at a period spanning from the earliest part of the twentieth century. Not bad. The ups and downs of the market (especially the stock market) are also referred to as the "bull" or "bear" markets. When we experience a bull market, the average price of stocks, bonds, and mutual funds tends to increase. During a bear market, prices decrease. Think of this as the bull market charging ahead and the bear market hibernating.

Now that you know some of the basics, it's time to start putting the pieces of this investment puzzle together. In the next chapter, we'll talk about building your own investment portfolio. This is the exciting part!

7

Get Investing, Part II:

OPTIONS AND STRATEGIES

In the previous chapter, you learned more about what investing is, why you should do it, and what type of investor you are. This knowledge is a powerful tool that will help you become a successful investor. In this chapter, we're going to get into some of the specific investment options and strategies available to you. This is the fun part!

Investment Options

A few years ago, I was teaching a "Dollars and Sense" course to an eighth-grade class. Throughout my presentation, I used the term "investment vehicle" a number of times. Near the end of the session, I asked the class to draw a picture or write a paragraph about what they learned throughout the day. I reviewed their work that evening and discovered a number of pictures of cars—cars on roads, cars in driveways, cars on top of mountains. Clearly, something had gotten lost in translation!

An investment vehicle is any type of investment you use to grow your money. Your investment portfolio is made up of a number of different investment vehicles. Some investment vehicles can even hold other vehicles—kind of like a car carrier! We'll get to the details in a few pages, but right now, let's take a look at the investment vehicles, or options, available to you. Knowing what they are and how they work will help you decide what options are best for you.

Investment Options

INVESTMENT TYPE	DESCRIPTION
Savings Account	A savings account is a regular bank account where you can safely store your money. In general, savings accounts pay very little interest, and are easy to access—a drawback when trying to save for the long term.
Stock	A stock is a certificate indicating ownership in a company. If the company is doing well, the value of your stock increases. If the company is not doing so well, the value of your stock will likely decrease. You can make money through stocks by either receiving regular income from dividends, or by selling the stock at a profit.
Bond	A bond is a certificate indicating that a company, an association, or a government has borrowed money from you. In return for making your funds available, the bond issuer will pay you a fixed amount of interest after a fixed period of time. Rates of return on bonds fluctuate with interest rates. Certain government bonds in the

	United States, Municipal Bonds, offer a tax incentive at the time of issuance.
Treasury Bill (T-bill)	A treasury bill is issued when a government borrows money from you and promises to pay it back, usually within one year. You do not gain interest on the money you lend the government. The bill is sold to you at a discounted rate, and purchased back at full value.
Certificate of Deposit (CD)	A CD is similar to a savings account, in that it's a very safe investment vehicle (you're guaranteed to get all your money back). But, unlike a savings account, you earn a decent rate of return. Your money is typically locked away for a period of time ranging from thirty days to five years. To fully benefit from the predetermined interest rate (either paid or compounded), don't cash your money out early.
Mutual Fund	A mutual fund is a professionally managed investment vehicle that pools money from many individuals, and invests it according to a common objective. It refers to a group of stocks, bonds, or an index. You buy units of the group, allowing you to own a little bit of many stocks, bonds, or an index. Although not guaranteed to make you money, they do provide a great opportunity to diversify your portfolio.
Index Fund	An index fund is a group of stocks pulled together to represent a specific part of the market, such as the S&P 500. Money invested is not guaranteed, although the opportunity to diversify is high.

Savings Accounts

A savings account can be a good place to keep your money, but only for the short term. Savings accounts are considered to be "liquid" investment opportunities, which means it's easy to get your hands on your cash. This is fine if you're using the account to store cash for things like groceries or rent, but it's not so good if you actually want to prevent yourself from spending! Also on the plus side, because you're effectively loaning the bank your money (they invest it, after all; it doesn't just sit there in the vault!), they pay you a small—very small!—amount of interest.

Perhaps the best thing about a savings account is it's a very safe place to keep your money. Through the Federal Deposit Insurance Corporation (FDIC), a deposit of up to $100,000 is guaranteed by the U.S. government in the event of loss or damage. Ensure your institution is covered by the FDIC so, unlike some of the other options we're going to discuss, your money is never really at risk.

Stocks

When you purchase stock, you're actually buying a piece of a corporation. You become a shareholder in that company—and you do so with the hope that the value of the corporation will increase, thereby increasing the value of your stock.

There are several ways you can make money on the stock market: You can sell your shares at a higher price than what you paid for them; you can receive a dividend (a payout to shareholders) from the corporation; or you can purchase more stock if and when the company decides to issue a new batch.

The prices of shares in companies vary widely. Some sell for as little as 50 cents (or lower), while others go for

$120 (or higher). Because you need to buy stocks through some type of financial institution or brokerage, all come with a transaction fee attached. Also, unlike your average savings account, the money you invest in stocks is never guaranteed, nor are you guaranteed any dividend payout.

Before you purchase any stock, do your research. Many people lose money on the stock market, because they have absolutely no information about the company in which they're investing. Others lose money because they've received a "hot tip" from a friend who may not know what they're talking about. Be smart, and dig around a bit. A corporation's risk level can be determined by looking into their history, and by examining the direction in which the company is heading. Read the financial section of your newspaper. Go online, and poke around the various investment sites.

If you know how to read a financial statement, you'll be able to assess a company's value potential. If you don't, consider consulting a financial adviser. One key thing you'll want to know is whether the company can afford to pay its short- and long-term debts. You can figure this out by dividing the company's current assets by its current liabilities to get the current ratio. The higher the current ratio, the more likely it is the company will be able to pay its bills in the short term. The general rule of thumb for many industries, not all, is if this figure is less than 1.2, the company may be in a bit of short-term trouble. Another trick is to calculate a debt-to-equity ratio (divide total liabilities by total equity) to see if the company can afford to pay their debts in the long term. Again, the general rule of thumb for many industries, not all, is if the number produced is greater than 2 or 3, the company may not be able to afford their debt payments over time.

Whatever you decide to do, make sure you approach stock-market investing with your eyes wide open. Even with ample research, it's possible to lose money on the stock market. Without investing, however, you're at an even greater disadvantage.

Why? The stock market has typically performed better than any other type of investment in the long run. Since 1970, the stock market (measured by the Standard & Poor's 500) has increased nearly 200 percent. The rate of return calculated by the S&P 500 index has been between 10 and 12 percent since the beginning of the last century. Savings rates tend to be much lower, like 0.5 to 3 percent. Let's assume you invested $1,000 in 1970 in a diversified stock-market portfolio. If you gained that 200 total percent average, the $1,000 you invested then would be worth nearly $200,000 today.

If you take the time to understand how it works, and what stocks are best for you, you can certainly do well over time.

Bonds

When a company or a government needs more money than it currently has, it may look to investors (like you!) for financial support. By issuing bonds, the company or government can find the capital it needs to stay in business. A bond states the borrower will pay a certain rate of return (interest rate) over the next few years or until the bond matures.

A bond makes investors money through the payment of interest. Some companies will issue a check every quarter (three months) to the investor for the amount of interest they've gained throughout that period. The amount varies depending on the amount of the bond and how many bonds the investor has. Other types of bonds don't issue interest checks at all. Instead, they wait until the bond matures. At that point, they pay back both the principal amount and the compounded interest.

When you purchase a bond, the issuer presents you with a certificate stating the name of the company or government, the dollar amount invested, interest rate promised, and maturity date. Typically, you must be at least eighteen to buy a bond through a broker, bank, or other financial institution. However, with the approval and support of a parent or guardian, you can usually proceed with the transaction.

There are three main types of bonds: government, municipal, and corporate.

- **Government bonds** tend to have secure rates of return, and are sold in a variety of denominations with the most common being $1,000. The maturity date is stated at the time of purchase, although the investor can usually cash in the bond prior to that date. A choice between compound or simple interest is often available. If you have the choice, take compound interest—it will make a big difference to the overall value of your portfolio.
- **Municipal bonds** are very similar to government bonds. The primary difference is that with municipal bonds, there are often tax incentives at the time of issuance to encourage an investor to invest in and support the municipality. For example, you can buy a municipal bond for the City of New York.

- **Corporate bonds** are almost identical to government bonds, although you'll likely need to put up more money to buy one. Bonds are generally considered a "safer" investment vehicle than stocks. Why? A bond is a corporation's written legal promise that it will repay a specified amount of money, with interest, after a specified amount of time. If the company happens to go bankrupt during that time, they're legally required to pay back anyone with a claim to the company's assets. No such promise exists with shareholders and stocks.

Although bonds are considered safe, there's also a downside to consider. The rate of return on a bond can be less than the rate of return you might receive on other investment vehicles—like mutual funds, stocks, and securities. However, if a corporation in a risky financial situation issues bonds, they often have to pay a higher rate of return to their investors. There is a tradeoff between risk and reward. As a general rule of thumb, less-risky investment vehicles pay lower rates of return, whereas riskier investments pay a higher return.

Bonds are best used as long-term investments. Maturity dates tend to be anywhere from five to thirty years after the date of issue. When the maturity date arrives, the bond will no longer earn interest. It is ready to be reinvested or cashed by the investor. If you want to cash your bond in early, there may be a penalty.

As with the stock market, you need to do your research before you buy. All bonds in the United States have a rating through the S&P or Moody's. The S&P Bond Rating System looks like this:

RATING	MEANING
AAA	High Credit Quality (Best Ones)
AA	Very Good Quality
A	Good Quality
BBB	Medium Quality
BB	Low–Medium Quality
B	Poor Quality
CCC	Sketchy Quality (Could miss payments)
CC	Very Sketchy Quality (Usually misses payments)
C	Extremely Sketchy Quality (Bankruptcy has been filed)
D	Default (The company is being forced to liquidate)
	Suspended Rating (Serious financial trouble)

Clearly, bonds with a CCC rating are considered a riskier investment than bonds with a AAA (triple A) rating. Taking this into account, a CCC-rated bond would likely feature a very attractive rate of return. However, if the issuing company slips into a D rating, you have to wait until the legal battles are settled before you get your money back. Even then, you might not receive all you invested. Be smart. Invest according to your risk tolerance.

Treasury Bills (T-Bills)

Unlike bonds, treasury bills are short-term investments, geared toward people who want to invest their money for ninety to 120 days. A treasury bill is issued when a government borrows money from you and promises to pay you back, usually within one year. Unlike with a bond, you don't gain interest on the money you lend. Instead, you lend your money at a discount and the government "tops you up" when the money is due to be returned. For example, you might buy a T-bill for $9,500 that's worth $10,000 on its maturity date. On the date of maturity you're paid $10,000. Typically, you can't get your money out of the T-bill until its maturity date.

The T-bill usually requires a large sum of money to invest—between $5,000 and $10,000 to start—making it an ideal place to stash cash for big-ticket items like cars, vacations, or down payments. The returns are moderate, but so is the risk. A T-bill can be purchased through a broker, bank, or other financial institution. Again, if you're under eighteen, you will likely need a parent or guardian to sign off on this purchase and act as the legal custodian for the assets (until you reach the age of eighteen in most states).

Certificates of Deposit (CDs)

A Certificate of Deposit (CD) is another good low-risk investment. Typically issued by your financial institution, the CD can be purchased for a minimum investment of $500 (although some institutions allow you to buy in via weekly or monthly plans for much less). The maturity terms can be anywhere from a few months to five years. As with bonds and T-bills, the rate of return on a CD is typically higher than what a savings account would offer, but lower than many other types of investments. However, the tradeoff is also the same: it's a less-risky investment because it's fully guaranteed.

One of the catches with the CD is your money is "locked in" until the maturity date (if you want it back earlier, there can be a penalty). Although some consider it a drawback, this feature actually makes the CD an excellent tool for individuals who are easily tempted to spend their money. It's also an ideal vehicle for investors hoping to make a big-ticket purchase within a few years.

Because the CD pays a relatively low interest rate, a young investor likely wouldn't want to keep all their money in CDs for the long term. Over the long run, stocks, bonds, and mutual funds will outperform a CD.

Mutual Funds

Back on page 112, we talked about investment vehicles containing other vehicles. That's a perfect description of a mutual fund. Another analogy that often works is a mutual fund is like an umbrella under which a number of diverse stock, bond, or investments are gathered.

A mutual fund is a group of stocks, bonds, or an index that a portfolio manager has chosen and crammed into a unit. The manager chooses the stocks with their clients' best interests in mind, and the stocks are generally similar in terms of their risk factor. When you buy one unit of a mutual fund, you're actually buying a little bit of every stock within that unit. It's a wonderful tool for investors looking to diversify and balance their portfolios.

A mutual fund has a greater potential to make money than T-bills, bonds, and CDs, but there is also more risk involved. Because you're dealing with the stock market, you're indirectly subject to its volatility. Mutual funds follow the market cycles very closely. When the markets are generally in a slump, your mutual funds are likely going to be worth less. When the markets are hot, your funds will be, too.

Mutual funds are categorized according to goals and risk levels. For example, a low-risk mutual fund would hold a grouping of low-risk stocks, bonds, or indexes. There are also growth funds (featuring higher-risk, higher-return investments), aggressive-growth funds, international funds, income-producing funds, and many more.

The mutual-fund market offers a wonderful opportunity for new investors. Unlike some other investment vehicles, mutual funds are cheap! While you may not be able to afford a significant quantity of stock, or a T-bill, you can invest in the stock market through mutual funds for $50 per month, and sometimes less. Think about that for a minute. Fifty dollars a month equals two dinners out with friends. Not a big investment, and a potentially high rate of return!

Mutual funds are best used as long-term investments. Ideally, investing in mutual funds until retirement gives you ample time to grow them. However, the shortest of the long-term time frames for mutual fund investment is likely closer to ten years. To receive the full benefit of a high rate of return, you must stick with your fund whether the markets are good or bad. If you hop from mutual fund to mutual fund, you end up missing out on their long-term-growth potential.

MUTUAL FUND FEES

Mutual fund managers are paid a yearly management fee also known as management expense ratio (MER). Usually, this is taken out of the fund itself, not your portfolio directly. The management fee is often a percentage of the earnings the fund makes throughout the year. It can be anywhere between 0.5 and 4 percent. Although some investors grumble about these fees, many others consider it a necessary expense. You are, in essence, paying for a service. Your fund manager is well educated and informed—just the kind of person to help you make good investment decisions.

Index Funds

Somewhat like mutual funds in terms of their umbrella quality, index funds (also called exchange-traded funds) allow you to buy a small piece of a large number of companies in the same industry or market. Index funds include those that track the major indexes (like the Dow Jones, or S&P 500), as well as funds that follow specific sectors (finance, technology, health). You can also purchase these funds through your financial institution, or your own self-managed investment account. Unlike mutual funds, index funds are usually managed by a computer and, therefore, have very limited management fees.

Although index funds have been around for a long while, they're still relatively underused. But that shouldn't scare you off. These investment vehicles are great for new investors. They're affordable, they allow for diversification within an industry, and they're not as risky as investing in stocks alone. One of the very best things about investing in index funds is you'll never under-perform the market (which has averaged between 10 and 12 percent since the early 1900s). This is because your fund is a representation of the market. If there's one disadvantage it's that you'll never outperform the market, either.

A good strategy when purchasing index funds is to look for industries (sectors) that are trending upward. For example, over the past few decades, the banking and financial services industry has consistently done well. To succeed with sector funds, it's important to catch the trends and ride them as if you were surfing on a wave. When one sector starts to slow, catch the next trend and ride it. To do this successfully, you need to keep current with what's going on in various industries. Beef up your business knowledge. It will pay off in the long run.

Investment Strategies

Now that you know what's available to you, and a little bit about how to use it, actually building your investment portfolio is the next step to financial success. In the following pages, you'll be introduced to some key investing strategies.

Many of the strategies presented here are not get-rich-quick schemes. Instead, they're based on sound investment advice that will carry you comfortably into your future. Sometimes you'll make money fast, other times, the growth will be slower. But ultimately, these are proven and successful long-term strategies.

Diversify and Balance

"Don't put all your eggs in one basket!" We've all heard this one before, haven't we? In terms of investing, this phrase cautions against putting all your money in one place. After all, if you lose that one basket, you've lost everything in it! However, if you diversify, the loss of one basket along the way won't be quite so devastating.

Another way to think about this is in terms of balance. That word—"balance"—will be a huge part of your financial life forever. It's crucial to success in investing (not to mention in your personal life!). Financially successful people learn how to balance spending, saving, investing, and giving back. In chapter 6, we looked at how important it is to create a portfolio that's well suited to your investment personality. But even the most well-defined investors need balance. Let's look at a few examples.

Amy is comfortable taking risks. As an eighteen-year-old student with plenty of support from her mom and dad, she knows she can afford to go after high-risk, high-yield investments. Amy has saved up her income from the past three summers, and has about $6,000 to invest. After lots of research and discussion with her parents, however, Amy knows she shouldn't risk everything. She wants to have some portion of her money in secure investments, just in case her aggressive/risky strategy takes a turn for the worst. So, she consults with a financial adviser at her local bank. After she shares her financial goals, they determine she would benefit most from a combination of growth-oriented investments and more conservative, less-risky investments. In the end, Amy's investment portfolio looks like this:

Amy's Portfolio for Aggressive Growth

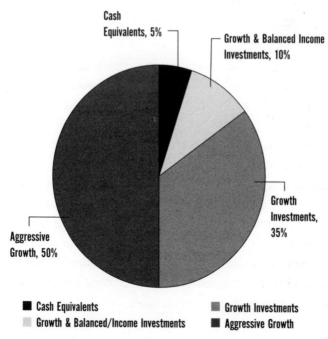

Cash Equivalents, 5%

Growth & Balanced Income Investments, 10%

Growth Investments, 35%

Aggressive Growth, 50%

■ Cash Equivalents   ■ Growth Investments
□ Growth & Balanced/Income Investments   ■ Aggressive Growth

Let me take a moment to explain the labels that appear on this graph. You're going to see them throughout this chapter. Simply put, they describe a few of the investment types available for Amy's needs.

- **Cash Equivalents:** These investments are very secure and very liquid (you can get your money out easily). Example: a savings account or T-bill.
- **Growth and Balanced-Income Investments:** These investments are a little more risky. They typically don't yield a huge return, yet they provide security. Example: a low-risk mutual fund, a CD, or low-risk stocks in very reputable companies.
- **Growth Investments:** These are even riskier. They will provide a higher yield and have a more-aggressive approach to making money. Example: a growth-oriented mutual fund, index fund, or stock in a company that's secure but in growth or expansion mode.
- **Aggressive Growth:** High-risk/high-reward investments. Example: hot stocks or high-risk mutual funds.

But what if you're not like Amy? What if all that risk makes you a little nervous? Juan, for example, knows he needs to be super careful with the $3,500 he's managed to save as he heads into university and beyond. He wants a good rate of return, but he simply can't afford to risk what he's managed to save so far. Based on his own research, he's decided to construct a portfolio mostly around safe investment vehicles. Juan's portfolio looks like this:

Juan's Portfolio for Conservative Growth

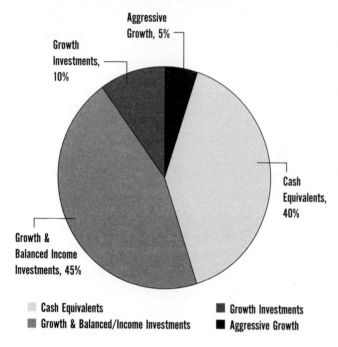

Most investors will likely fall somewhere between Amy and Juan on the risk scale. And that's just fine. Whatever your desired rate of return, you can combine your types of investments so they can give you that kind of return. Let's look at one more example.

Twenty-six-year-old Andrea has some money to invest, but she isn't sure she wants a whole lot of risk. After talking to an adviser at the bank, she decided to take advantage of her youth, and ability to weather the market. Based on her adviser's recommendation, Andrea knows she'd like to earn a return of between 8 and 10 percent over the long run—what investors typically call "balanced growth." Andrea's portfolio might look something like this:

Andrea's Portfolio for Balanced Growth

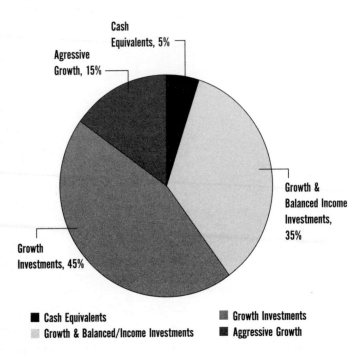

Whatever your combination, your ultimate goal is to have an investment bundle that meets your needs. Like Amy, you might be willing to tolerate a certain amount of risk. Or perhaps you're more conservative, like Juan. Chances are good that a fair number of you will fall into Andrea's territory—ready to invest, but not ready to risk it all. Talk to an adviser at your local bank. Take Andrea's sample portfolio with you. Don't be afraid to ask questions—even ones you think sound dumb. You have enough knowledge now to ensure you get what you need out of the various investment options available to you. Use it!

Dollar-Cost Averaging

Once you've got the diversification and balance thing down, and you've chosen the right investment vehicles for you, you can start thinking about how to maximize your investment dollars. Dollar-cost averaging is one really neat trick. Simply defined, it means making a contribution to some type of investment plan on a regular basis. For example, you may contribute $30 a month from your job earnings, or your allowance. Over time, you buy $30 each month of that investment, say a mutual fund. Due to changes in the market, the cost of that mutual fund fluctuates—sometimes the cost may be low, sometimes higher. By purchasing regularly, you're taking advantage of the fund's average cost, buying more units when the cost is low, and less when the cost is high. And regardless of the cost, you still experience the benefits of compounded interest.

Some investors think saving up and contributing one lump sum of money will be the best way to invest. They often wait around for the prices of their desired investments to decrease so they're cheaper to buy. All the while, they're missing out on the advantages of being in the market the entire time. It's hard to time the market. You don't want to be waiting around with thousands of dollars to invest, earning zero interest on the sum.

Dollar-cost averaging allows investors to be in the market at all times, taking advantage of both its highs and lows. Here's how it works. Let's say Jason is investing in a mutual fund called xyz Fund. The average monthly prices are listed in the chart below. If Jason invests once per month, his average cost of buying the mutual fund is $55.91:

MONTH	PRICE
January	$50.25
February	$52.36
March	$60.13
April	$55.12
May	$61.11
June	$60.01
July	$57.63
August	$55.68
September	$54.89
October	$54.23
November	$55.62
December	$53.89
Average Price	$55.91

If Jason tried to time the market and hold onto his investment dollars until he thought the time was right, he might end up paying more or less than this average. Perhaps he'd decide, after watching XYZ Fund drop in value between May and July, it wasn't going to go any lower. Not only would he be wrong, but he'd end up paying more than the average cost over a year. Investing regularly makes sense.

Always Take Free Money

If you're working at a full-time job (nowadays even a part-time job), you may have access to a compensation plan that includes a self-directed retirement account. Often, these plans allow you to contribute to the plan a certain percentage or dollar value of your pretax pay (taken straight off your paycheck). Some companies will even help you save money by matching a percentage of your contributions. Let's say your company agrees to match your contribution, up to $50 a month. This means if you contribute $50, an additional $50 will be deposited into your savings plan (if you put in $40, your employer will put in $40). Your employer may not match your contribution equally, but free money is free money. Take it! Even better, your money and the money your employer has contributed will all earn interest. Short of winning the lottery, it doesn't get any better than that!

There are two common self-directed retirement accounts you should look into and which most employers offer:

- 401(k): The 401(k) is the most common account offered by companies, that helps you save money for your retirement. These plans allow you to group different investment options together into one plan. The government will allow you to deduct the amount you save from your taxable income. (See chapter 8 for more information.)
- 403(b): The 403(b) is the equivalent account, but is offered only to employees who work for schools, hospitals, not-for-profits, and the like.

The benefits of these plans again are:

1) they allow you to invest pretax dollars (an example of this benefit is found later in chapter 8)
2) they take your contribution out automatically, so you can't spend your retirement savings
3) some employers will help you save by matching a percentage of your contribution

4) you'll earn compound interest in your account; and

5) you can set these plans up for free

Prepare for the Long Haul (or Don't Buy High and Sell Low)

Looking down the road of life, what does "the long haul" mean to you? Fifty years? Forty? Thirty-five? It's worth thinking about for a moment. Here's why:

Over the past century, the mutual-fund and stock markets have averaged a return of 10 to 12 percent. Many investors, however, don't reap the benefits of that excellent rate of return. Instead, they average less than a 4 percent return. Why? Investors earning less than 4 percent are those who keep changing and shuffling their portfolio. When the market environment changes, they get scared—buying new investment options, selling old ones. Regardless of what they're doing, they're usually doing it at precisely the wrong time, probably because they're letting their emotions prevail.

Those emotions work like this. When the markets are performing poorly, the overall value of your portfolio tends to decrease. In response, you might find yourself getting a little antsy and nervous—after all, you're not making money; you may even be losing money! So what do you do? Well, you might pull money out of your investments, thinking you'll save yourself from further losses. Actually, you're pulling out when you'll get the least amount of money for your investments. Making matters worse, you might decide to reinvest when the markets take a turn back up. Now, however, the price of investing has increased and you'll be paying more than you should!

This emotional reaction is the complete opposite of a profitable strategy. You're buying high and selling low. If you keep doing this, you won't be making anywhere near the historical 10 to 12 percent I mentioned above. You'll be right around the 4 percent mark instead, which barely beats the rate of inflation.

If you find yourself tempted to tamper, remember this key piece of investment knowledge: to make money with investments, you must leave your money in place for the long haul. Avoid tampering. Tampering costs you money! When your investment statements arrive, look at them quickly and then put them aside. You can examine them in more detail once a year, but you shouldn't need to do it any more often. A lot can happen in a year and changes may cause you to change your investment strategy. For example, if you had a baby, got married, or bought a house, you might want to review your investments/strategies.

Markets change, and so do trends. Markets go up and down, depending on a number of factors. But you have to ride the ups and downs like everyone else. Ensure you review your strategies, and keep in mind that investing for financial success is a long-term process.

Dividend Strategies

In my final year of university, one of my class groups developed a dividend signaling strategy as part of a course project. We started with the assumption that a corporation's dividend policy has significant signaling implications. Some investors use dividend signaling as a way to analyze the overall health of a company. There is a substantial amount of evidence suggesting an increase in dividends is viewed positively by the market, while a decrease is understood to be a negative signal. After all, when a company sends out a dividend, it's indicating it has the money to do so. A dividend reduction sends the opposite message: perhaps this company is in need of cash. We wanted our mock portfolio to produce positive returns based on dividend signals.

Our strategy was to buy shares in companies that increased their dividend amounts. We held our position in firms with a stable dividend. We sold a portion of our position when firms decreased their dividend amount. Overall, our sample portfolio of forty-six American companies, paying regular dividends, outperformed the benchmark. We even ran the portfolio through recessionary trends in the early part of this decade (the Technology Bubble). Throughout the five-year period we tracked our strategy, our average rate of return per year was 14.44 percent. Our benchmark return was negative through most of those same five years. We were making money, while others were not.

Although the implementation of this strategy requires a lot of research, much purchasing and selling of stocks, and a significant amount of money to cover transaction fees, it's still a lower-risk, stable, and fruitful investment opportunity. If you're interested in giving it a try, you might consider buying into a mutual fund that invests in dividend-paying stocks. This is sometimes referred to as a dividend mutual fund (almost every institution selling mutual funds has one).

Be Willing to Leverage

If you had enough money available to purchase a big-ticket item, would you use it? Of course, right? Wrong. Some people actually take out loans for certain items, even when the necessary money is available. And no, those people are not crazy. Sometimes, borrowing money to make money makes sense. It's called leveraging.

Let's say you've saved up $5,000 for the purchase of your first used car. You've even found a really great deal on a car with all the features you wanted. You figure you'll just pay for the car outright, but when you go to the bank to get a certified check, your financial adviser tells you about a combination of mutual funds that are expected to earn 10.5 percent over a three-year period. She tries to convince you to invest your $5,000 in this portfolio, rather than putting it all down on the car.

Now you're torn! You want to buy the car, but earning 10.5 percent on your $5,000 sounds pretty good, too. Luckily, your banker tells you how you can do both through leveraging. The bank is willing to lend you the $5,000 to buy your car at a reasonable 7 percent interest rate. You'll have three years to pay back the loan. At the same time, she'll invest the $5,000 you've already saved in the mutual fund portfolio that's expected to earn 10.5 percent. Because you're earning a higher rate of return than you'll be spending on interest, you're actually making money. In fact, your relative overall rate of return after the three-year period is 3.5 percent (10.5 minus 7).

Are you interested in knowing how much profit you can actually make if everything goes according to plan? (Remember, it's not a straight calculation of interest on the principal amount invested, because interest would be compounded annually.) A handy calculation called the "future value formula" will show you: $P \times (1 + i)^n$. P is principal invested; i is interest rate; and n is investment period: principal multiplied by one plus the interest rate to the exponent of time. If you're head is already pounding, don't worry. This is actually a pretty simple formula you can plug into any spreadsheet. You don't have to do it in your head!

In the case of you and your car/mutual funds, this is what you need to know: the principal amount invested is $5,000. The interest rate is 3.5 percent (in the world of formulas, you have to write this as 0.035 because it's a small part of one whole). The length of time over which the money is being invested is three years. In other words,

$$\$5,000 \times (1 + 0.035)^3 = \$5,543.59$$

To discover how much money you actually made using this leveraging technique, just subtract the $5,000 you borrowed from the number above. The grand total is $543.59. Not bad. (If you want to get really fancy, why not consider adding a regular monthly contribution to your initial sum? You'll end up growing your money even more!)

There's one thing to watch out for when using the leverage technique: You do have to make monthly payments on the borrowed money. In the example above, you'd likely be paying close to $150 a month toward your loan. If you can afford to do this, you'll make some decent money a few years down the road.

Call in the Dogs

The Dogs of the Dow (referring to the Dow Jones) strategy was formulated in 1972. Since then, it has proven to be very profitable for those who have followed it. The basic idea is you purchase your investments when the prices are low and sell them when the prices are high. Makes sense, right? The strategy is implemented by purchasing approximately ten stocks from the exchange. The stocks you buy are those with the highest dividend yield at the beginning of the year. These will likely be low in price (hence the term "dogs"), because the payment of a dividend decreases the amount of cash available to the business. Less cash means less value on the books. The idea here is you purchase these stocks "cheap" and watch them grow to become more valuable.

KNOW YOUR LIMIT

A good financial strategy needs to take your personal limits into account. It's important to know when and if you've made enough (or lost enough) money. You'll need to set your own personal standard, so you can be satisfied with your portfolio of investments. For example, perhaps a 20 percent return works for you. If you're fortunate enough to make a 20 percent return on a stock or another investment, you'll be ready to sell. Or, perhaps, you'll set your loss limit at 20 percent. It's possible you'll want to alter your personal limits based on changing circumstances and market conditions, but it's worthwhile to think about a starting point before you dive into investing. I'd recommend consulting a reputable financial adviser to come up with a reasonable goal for your returns.

Look for Value

With a value-investing strategy, the investor looks to invest in "beaten down" and undervalued companies. Understand and pay close attention to businesses that have been hit by short-term struggles. Ask yourself if the company can overcome the problem. If you think they can (and the research supports this), then you may be able to take advantage of lower share prices. For example, Research in Motion (makers of the BlackBerry®) was having patent problems just a few years ago. If you invested in RIM at that time, you would have saved 20 to 30 percent on their share price. Another good example might be a clothing outfitter facing a huge increase in demand. If they don't have enough inventory on hand to meet the initial orders, their share price might drop in value. If they can overcome this short-term inventory struggle, they can and will experience growth. If you choose to try your hand at this strategy, ensure you do your research. Newspapers, magazines, and online financial sites can be wonderful sources of information.

INVEST IN WHAT YOU KNOW

Peter Lynch is a famous investor who uses the buy-and-hold strategy described in the "Long Haul" section on page 132. Another key to his success is his "invest in what you know" approach. With this strategy, you simply invest in companies you know a lot about. For example, a young professional might invest in Sony, Honda, or Disney. All of these companies are visibly recognizable. As well, researching things that interest you is never difficult or boring!

8

Get Specific:

HOMES, KIDS, AND STUFF LIKE THAT

This chapter deals with specific situations that may or may not apply to you right now. However, at some point in your life, these things (education, house-hunting, retirement, even children) may be very relevant. For example, if you're sixteen and in high school, you might not be thinking about kids or houses just yet. However, if you're nearing the end of your university degree, you might be considering purchasing a home in the near future. If you're married or engaged, and thinking about children, you might be interested in saving for your children's education. Nevertheless, one thing remains true: everyone—regardless of life situation—should be thinking about their financial future and retirement.

Education

Marla wants to go to university to become a teacher. She's aware her education costs will be somewhere between $10,000 and $20,000 per year. Unfortunately, her parents are not in a position to help her out. Although Marla has heard horror *stories about student loans, she's beginning to wonder if they might be the only answer to her dilemma.*

Most investment books don't include strategies designed to help pay for education—but, then again, most investment books aren't written for people under thirty! But what if, like Marla, you're facing the challenge of paying for your own education? You're not alone. Only a handful of people are lucky enough to go to school debt-free. Most students rely on lines of credit or student loans to get through. With a four-year degree costing an average of $40,000 to $60,000 today, many young American graduates have between $20,000 and $30,000 in student debt.

If you know in advance you'll have to pay for your own education, you might want to consider a stacked-CD strategy. Back in chapter 7, we learned CDs are certificates of deposit. Whatever you invest is guaranteed to stay safe and earn at least some interest, while it's invested for a specified period of time. Most importantly, CDs have different maturity dates. So, you could invest in a CD and have it mature anywhere from thirty days to five years from now. A stacked-CD strategy is sort of like a forced savings plan. It involves investing in CDs both before going to school and throughout school. With proper planning, you can ensure one CD will mature every year or semester throughout your postsecondary school career—effectively releasing a handy sum of money to assist you in paying for tuition and books.

Let's use Marla, from the case study above, to show us how this can work. In the summer between tenth and eleventh grade, Marla gets a part-time job, maybe at a golf course. Since she's working full time throughout her summer break, she manages to make about $3,000. Because she's still living at home with her mom and dad—who pay the mortgage, the bills, and for all her food—Marla manages to save $2,000 from her earnings. At the end of the summer, she visits the bank, speaks to an adviser, and purchases a CD with a decent rate of return and a two-year term. That means it will mature during her first year of post-secondary education, if she goes to college right after high school.

The following summer, between eleventh and twelfth grade, Marla works at the same job and saves another $2,000. Once again, she visits the bank at the end of August, and purchases another two-year CD with a decent rate of return. This means when she's about to start her second year of post-secondary school, her second CD will be maturing.

See? If Marla continued with this pattern of saving and investing in a CD every summer, she'd end up "stacking" her CDs (see the chart below), so they matured at the beginning of each year of post-secondary school. I know, I know! First-hand experience has certainly taught me that $2,000 isn't enough to pay for a full year of post-secondary education, but it's $2,000 more than you'd have if you didn't invest, and it certainly puts a dent in those tuition costs!

YEAR 1	YEAR 2	YEAR 3	YEAR 4	YEAR 5	YEAR 6	YEAR 7
$2,000 invested at 4%		$2,163.20				
	$2,000 invested at 4%		$2,163.20			
		$2,000 invested at 4%		$2,163.20		
			$2,000 invested at 4%		$2,163.20	
				$2,000 invested at 4%		$2,163.20

New Dollars Invested
Maturity Value

Another thing to note: When Marla starts university or college, she can take advantage of the fact summer break is longer, sometimes two months longer. She can work more, earn more, save more, and purchase more valuable CDs. A good deal all around!

THE COSTS AND VALUE OF EDUCATION

Have you ever wondered how much it really costs you to go to school? The average total cost of a four-year undergraduate degree in the United States is approximately $50,000—and this doesn't necessarily include living expenses, or purchasing a computer and software! But it doesn't end there. Because you're in school, you give up the opportunity to work full time and make some money. Let's say you could count on an annual salary of $30,000. Over the course of your four-year degree, you'd be "losing" a potential $120,000. Add that to the $50,000 you're spending on tuition and books, and your post-secondary education is "costing" you $170,000!

Are you asking yourself why you should bother? The answer is because over the course of your lifetime, you'll make at least *double* the income of someone without a post-secondary education. Your career choices (Remember chapter 1? Choice equals freedom) will be better and more varied, and your income greater. It's worth noting when we refer to post-secondary education, we're not talking exclusively about colleges and universities. Throughout North America, there's a huge demand for trades. Students pursuing this path have to go through extensive apprenticeship programs, courses, and testing. Post-secondary education is no longer limited to degrees. Certificates, apprenticeships, working terms, and other options are also included.

Home, Sweet Home

Krista is a twenty-one-year-old student in her first year of university. She wants to move out of her suburban family home as soon as she's finished her post-secondary education. She is currently paying for her tuition and books, and is wondering how she's going to afford a down payment. She has her heart set on a condo nearer to the city center—close to her friends and potential employment opportunities.

Over the past twenty years, the North American condo market has exploded. Developers are targeting almost every demographic group, although "under thirties" seem to be the focus of much condo advertising. Why? Condos are typically less expensive than detached homes. They are easy to care for and manage. They offer young people a perfect way to enter the real-estate market, without being completely strapped for cash.

First-time home buyers face significant challenges when they enter the real-estate market. Not only do they need to come up with a down payment to own a home—whether it's a townhouse, condo, or house—they'll also need to get a mortgage. A mortgage is a long-term debt instrument used to pay for your home. It's like having a contract stating a certain property, your home, will be pledged as security against the value of the loan. So, if you don't make your payments, the bank will take your house. Mortgages often take fifteen to thirty years to pay off. This may sound scary but, in fact, a mortgage is very beneficial in the long run. American home owners are nearly thirty times wealthier than people who rent for their entire lives. Purchasing a home is one of the best long-term investments you can make.

Before we learn about how you go about purchasing a home, it's critical we look at the real estate market overall. Interestingly, the market has exploded over the course of the last few decades. Nowadays, it's not uncommon for a tiny, basic condo in New York City to fetch a price of over $350,000. Housing prices climbed steadily through the early 1990s. However, in late 2006, this steamy hot market started to cool off a bit. Many people have been throwing around the term "real-estate bubble," equating the slowing of the real-estate market to the "dot com bubble." Before you get excited about the market crashing, it's important to remember something: Real estate has proven to be a very sound investment in the long term—far better than throwing money out the window by paying rent on a monthly basis. Through the ups and downs of the market, real estate has returned just over 6 percent since 1968 according to the National Association of Realtors.

Regardless of what's happening right now in the real-estate market, keep a long-term perspective in mind when you plan on purchasing real estate. This section will also give you some tools to weather the storm so you can properly position yourself in the real-estate market, regardless of its current condition.

So, how do you go about it? Well, you could start socking away money for that down payment in your checking account, or hide your cash in a safety deposit box until you're ready to make the purchase. But, at this stage, you know these approaches aren't going to get you very far. Sure, you might gain some interest over the years, but you might also dip into your savings from time to time. All in all, these are terrible ways to save your money for a long-term, big-ticket item.

Remember Krista from the case study above? Well, she's actually in pretty good shape. She has two things going for her: she knows what she wants, and she's willing to figure out a way to make it happen. Because she has some time on her side—three to five years in school— she'll want to ensure she's earning interest on the money she invests, and she'll want to make sure she can't touch that money (and accidentally ruin her long-term dreams because of one fabulous pair of shoes!). It wouldn't hurt, either, for Krista to look for ways she can grow her down payment while in the savings process.

The very first thing Krista needs to do is visit her financial institution. Taking into account local laws, interest rates, her FICO score, and other personal financial circumstances, an adviser will be able to determine how much money she needs to save to cover a down payment. The typical first-time home buyer can finance up to 95, 97, or 100 percent of the purchase price of their home. If you can't come up with 20 percent of the cost of your home for a down payment, you'll have to pay this thing called *private mortgage insurance* (PMI). Most "under thirties" are strapped for cash, and end up with a down payment of less than 20 percent. Let's say you're interested in putting in a 3 percent down payment on a place costing $175,000. This down payment would be approximately $5,250.

In Krista's scenario, let's assume she takes either three, four, or five years to save her money for a down payment. Let's also assume she's choosing to save from 3 to 25 percent of the value of the home. Have a look at the table below to find out how much money she'll have to save every month without accrued interest.

KRISTA'S SAVINGS PER MONTH	3% DOWN $5,250	5% DOWN $8,750	10% DOWN $17,500	15% DOWN $26,250	20% DOWN $35,000	25% DOWN $43,750
3 Years (36 months)	$145.83	$243.06	$486.11	$729.17	$972.22	$1,215.28
4 Years (48 months)	$109.38	$182.29	$364.58	$546.88	$729.17	$911.46
5 Years (60 months)	$87.50	$145.83	$291.67	$437.50	$583.33	$729.17

But what if Krista starts saving her money in a high-interest savings account with compound interest, or in a CD with compound interest? Both investments are very safe and secure, so Krista won't have to worry about putting her down payment at risk. And she'll likely fetch a rate of return of 2 to 4 percent compounded annually, which would help her reach her savings goal sooner than she expected. Krista could also explore money-market mutual funds, though they're not guaranteed. However, these funds invest in the safest, most secure securities, like short-term government bonds. With all the above savings options, she should shop around for the most competitive interest rates.

Let's assume Krista decides to save for a 10 percent down payment of $17,500, give or take a few pennies and decimal places, over the course of three, four, or five years with an investment rate of return of 3 percent.

Over three years:

YEARS	SAVED PER YEAR	MONTHLY SAVINGS 10% DOWNPAYMENT	TOTAL SAVED	SAVED WITH INTEREST	SAVINGS INTEREST RATE
1	$5,833.32	$486.11	$ 5,833.32	$ 6,008.32	3%
2	$5,833.32	$486.11	$11,666.64	$12,196.89	3%
3	$5,833.32	$486.11	$17,499.96	$18,571.12	3%

Over four years (and with lower monthly savings):

YEARS	SAVED PER YEAR	MONTHLY SAVINGS 10% DOWNPAYMENT	TOTAL SAVED	SAVED WITH INTEREST	SAVINGS INTEREST RATE
1	$4,374.96	$364.58	$ 4,374.96	$ 4,506.21	3%
2	$4,374.96	$364.58	$ 8,749.92	$ 9,147.60	3%
3	$4,374.96	$364.58	$13,124.88	$13,928.24	3%
4	$4,374.96	$364.58	$17,499.84	$18,852.30	3%

Over five years (and with lower monthly savings):

YEARS	SAVED PER YEAR	MONTHLY SAVINGS 10% DOWNPAYMENT	TOTAL SAVED	SAVED WITH INTEREST	SAVINGS INTEREST RATE
1	$3,500.04	$291.67	$ 3,500.04	$ 3,605.04	3%
2	$3,500.04	$291.67	$ 7,000.08	$ 7,318.23	3%
3	$3,500.04	$291.67	$10,500.12	$11,142.82	3%
4	$3,500.04	$291.67	$14,000.16	$15,082.15	3%
5	$3,500.04	$291.67	$17,500.20	$19,139.65	3%

As you can see, time really is on Krista's side. With a little forethought and planning, she should have no trouble making her dream a reality!

Getting Aggressive: Mortgage-Rate Shopping and the Possibility of Leveraging

If you're fortunate enough to have saved a solid down payment for your home, and have already found your dream home, you should take a very aggressive approach to your next house-buying step—mortgage-rate shopping.

As with any other purchase, you want to be very certain you're getting the best value for your dollar. When it comes to mortgage rates, even 0.5 percent can make a huge difference in your monthly mortgage payments. Below is a table with monthly mortgage payments rounded to the nearest dollar for a thirty-year amortization period.

Monthly Mortgage Payment with a Thirty-Year Amortization

Rate	100,000 (monthly payment)	150,000 (monthly payment)	200,000 (monthly payment)	250,000 (monthly payment)	300,000 (monthly payment)
5.00%	$537	$ 805	$1,074	$1,342	$1,610
5.50%	$568	$ 852	$1,136	$1,419	$1,703
6.00%	$600	$ 899	$1,199	$1,499	$1,799
6.50%	$632	$ 948	$1,264	$1,580	$1,896
7.00%	$665	$ 998	$1,331	$1,663	$1,996
7.50%	$699	$1,049	$1,398	$1,748	$2,098
8.00%	$734	$1,101	$1,468	$1,834	$2,201

It's also important to consider the power of leveraging (see chapter 7) when you're about to purchase a home. Paul has been very lucky. Thanks to a sizable gift from his grandmother, and some hard work at jobs both during the summer and throughout the school year, Paul has managed to save $60,000 toward a down payment. The condo he's set his sights on costs $120,000. The bank has already told Paul he can put down as little as 0, 3, or 5 percent to secure the unit he wants. Paul knows the more he puts down, the lower his monthly payments will be. However, he's reluctant to part with all his hard-earned money. Therefore, he's tossing around the idea of putting down either 5 percent ($6,000), or his entire $60,000, which would be 50 percent of the condo's purchase price.

Before he makes any hard and fast decisions, Paul should take a good look at the interest rate the bank is offering. Again, if Paul's FICO score is healthy (760 or higher), his interest rate will be very low when compared to the interest rate offered to someone with a score in the 500 zone. This difference in FICO scores can be equal to more than $100,000 over the life of a thirty-year mortgage. If it's a good rate (fairly low), he might want to consider making his down payment as small as possible. Using this strategy, Paul would put down a small amount on his home, invest the larger portion of his cash, and let the interest from his investments compound and grow.

Let's crunch some numbers and see how this works. Remember, Paul has saved $60,000, the condo costs $120,000, the bank and Paul have agreed to a 5 percent down payment, or $6,000. If he only put $6,000 down, he'd be left with a mortgage of $114,000, and $54,000 to invest elsewhere (for simplicity's sake, we're going to leave closing costs, private mortgage insurance, and other related fees out of the equation).

Let's say Paul finds an investment portfolio expected to return 8 percent annually. Remember the future-value-of-money formula (see chapter 7): $P \times (1 + i)^n$ (P is principal invested; i is interest rate; n is investment period). In Paul's case, the formula works out like this:

$$\$54,000 \times (1 + 0.08)^1 = \$58,320$$

This means Paul can put his $54,000 into that investment vehicle and, in one year's time, he'll have earned $4,320 in return ($58,320 − $54,000). He can now use that $4,320 to help pay off his mortgage, or he could compound it back into his investment and grow his money even more.

The basic idea is this—if Paul can take advantage of a low interest rate on his mortgage—lower than what he's making on his investments (8 percent), he'll come out on top. For example, if he's paying 5.5 percent on his mortgage, and making 8 percent on his investment portfolio, then theoretically he's ahead by 2.5 percent (8 − 5.5 = 2.5). If the markets are performing quite poorly, he might end up making less than 8 percent on his portfolio in the short run. If his rate of return on his investment portfolio was 4 percent, and his mortgage rate remains at 5.5 percent, he's paying a greater amount of interest on his mortgage. Therefore, it's in his best interest to place the additional money on the mortgage. There are a number of factors playing into this scenario. For example, the value of homes in certain areas of the country has increased substantially over the long run.

Getting Aggressive: Shopping for the Best Mortgage Structure

The next important piece of the mortgage process is shopping for the best mortgage structure to suit your needs.

These days, homeowners typically stay put for about five to seven years, then they move on to another home. Lenders have designed a few primary mortgage structures to address your needs and your stage of life.

First, if you've found your dream home and don't plan on selling or moving for a long time (more than about ten years), you benefit most from a fifteen-year or thirty-year fixed-rate mortgage. This is a fairly conservative mortgage structure because the rate stays the same for the entire fifteen- or thirty-year life of the loan. Because your interest rate is locked in, your payments never change and you're protected if and when interest rates increase. The primary difference between the two is in the amortization period, which is the length of time it takes to pay back the loan. Since it will take longer to pay back a thirty-year mortgage, the payments are lower. The fifteen-year mortgage takes less time to pay off, so your payments will be higher. The interest rate on a thirty-year mortgage is a little higher than a fifteen-year mortgage, typically, by 0.5 percent.

The next mortgage structure works best for people who have no intention of staying in their home for more than a couple of years. The adjustable-rate mortgage offers an interest rate of 1 to 2 percentage points below a fixed-rate mortgage, thus reducing monthly payments. However, the rate is adjusted every six months to a year (sometimes even monthly). That can put a young person in a pretty sticky position, if rates hike upward. However, if you have very short-term plans to stay put, and can handle a little bit of risk, you can really benefit from this structure when interest rates are low.

The last primary mortgage structure is a bit of a hybrid between the fixed-rate and the adjustable-rate mortgages. This structure is known as the intermediate adjustable-rate or hybrid mortgage. This structure works well for people who initially want stability, but also know the approximate time frame of when they'll want to buy a different home and move. The way it works is the first part of this loan is fixed, so your payments are the same each month. Then, after three, five, seven or ten years, the interest rate becomes adjustable, either annually or every six months. This structure offers a lower rate than a thirty-year or fifteen-year fixed-rate mortgage. However, the risk associated with this structure is that once the rate is adjusted, your payments could increase. For most young "under thirties" this structure makes sense, seeing as we often plan on moving a number of times before we find our dream home. It allows us to take advantage of lower rates, thus lower payments, which are stable at the beginning of our home-ownership experience. These mortgages have symbols attached to them like 3/1, 5/1, 7/1, or 10/1. You would read 3/1 as three years fixed with the interest rate being adjustable every year after that three years is up.

There are so many mortgage structures available to a young person. However, try not to get sucked into the zero-down or interest-only mortgages. The zero-down mortgage worries me because you haven't saved for a down payment. The process of saving for a down payment will help you adjust—in advance—to being a home owner, which is a lot of financial responsibility. Though it gets you out of the renting situation quickly, you need to have discipline and healthy financial habits to borrow large sums of money. Lenders in North America know this is a risky structure, and some will charge you increased interest rates or fees to shoulder this risk. Try to save at least 3 to 5 percent before you think of buying a house.

The most frightening mortgage is the interest-only structure, in which you only pay the interest part of your mortgage for up to ten or fifteen years. At that point, you must pay back the principal and remaining interest over the outstanding amortization period. For example, if you take out a thirty-year mortgage, you would pay interest only for the first ten years and your initial payments would be small. However, after that ten-year period is over, your payments skyrocket because you now have to pay back both the principal and interest in the remaining twenty years. We're likely talking about a payment that increases by *hundreds* of dollars each month. This can be a very tight payment schedule.

The idea behind this mortgage structure is that throughout the initial years, while you're paying just the interest portion, the value of your home will appreciate. You would then be able to refinance, come up with the 20 percent needed to convert to a conventional loan, and come out ahead of the game. The problem with this structure is that it's too risky. Who knows exactly where the real-estate market will be in 10 or 15 years? Who knows whether your home will appreciate in value enough to make the conversion? In addition to this risk, if you end up being unable to refinance and make the conversion, you're left making huge principal and interest payments that could break you if your income and circumstances can't handle it.

You Have Support When Buying a Home

Did you know the government actually wants to help you purchase a home? Yes, this is indeed true. In 2002, the American government made it quite clear they wanted to increase the number of Americans owning homes by over five million people throughout the course of eight years. The government's strategic initiative has drawn attention to a number of agencies and organizations that help people—of all ages, income brackets, and walks of life—buy homes. If you want to know how the government can help you, contact the following agencies:

- National Council of State Housing Agencies (www.ncsha.org)
- U.S. Department of Housing and Urban Development (www.hud.gov)
- Freddie Mac (www.freddiemac.com)
- Fannie Mae (www.fanniemae.com)

If you need more information on buying a home and/or mortgages, visit your local financial institution or check out some of the following Web sites:

- www.bankrate.com
- www.homebuyingguide.org
- www.bankofamerica.com
- www.jpmorganchase.com
- www.citigroup.com
- www.wachovia.com

Retirement Savings: 401(k), 403(b), IRA, and Roth IRA

401 (k) and 403 (b)

I introduced the 401(k) and 403(b) plans in the previous chapter. They're self-directed retirement savings plans you can set up with your employer. Again, the benefits of these plans are:

- They allow you to invest pretax dollars (an example of this benefit is found below).
- They take your contribution out automatically, so you can't spend your retirement savings.
- Some employers will help you save by matching a percentage of your contribution.
- You'll earn compound interest in your account.
- You can set these plans up for free.

Here's an example of how these 401(k) or 403(b) plans can work for you. Let's say Alan makes $30,000 a year as a marketing assistant, and doesn't use the 401(k) plan available to him at his work. Instead, Alan invests 10 percent of his gross annual income ($3,000), with after-tax dollars. Knowing the average American pays 30 percent of their income to Uncle Sam, 30 percent of Alan's gross pay is $9,000, which reduces his leftover income to $21,000. Out of that remaining $21,000, he invests $3,000, which means he only has $18,000 left to spend each year on things like rent, a cell phone, groceries, and other things. Saving $3,000 annually means he'll have to save $250 per month.

Paula, on the other hand, works in the same department, makes $30,000 per year, but uses the 401(k) plan at work. If Paula saves 10 percent of her gross annual income (so $3,000) with pretax dollars, she ends up paying taxes on $27,000 worth of income, whereas Alan paid taxes on the full $30,000. So, Paula will be taxed 30 percent of $27,000 which equates to $8,100 paid in taxes. That's a full $900 less in tax, when compared to Alan. The income Paula has left over is $18,900.

In both scenarios, Alan and Paula save $3,000. However, in Paula's scenario, her leftover income is $18,900, whereas Alan's leftover income is only $18,000. For Paula, that means she'll have an extra $900 per year to spend, or $75 per month.

Remarkably, only one in four Americans uses these plans. If the above example doesn't convince you to sign up, maybe this will. Let's say Paula and Alan's employer has committed to matching 50 percent of employee savings *if* they use the 401(k) plan. That would mean Paula would have saved $3,000, and her employer would have added an additional $1,500 in savings to her plan. In essence, this is like getting a raise. Alan, who invests outside the plan, will not reap the benefits of his employer matching his contributions. I hope the continuation of this example convinces you to take the initiative, sign up, and maximize the use of the 401(k) or 403(b) plan at your work. Again, to wrap this all up, free money rocks and you should take it.

Below are the contribution limits for the 401(k), 403(b) and 457 (similar to the first two) plans:

YEAR	MAXIMUM ALLOWABLE (AGE 49 OR YOUNGER)	MAXIMUM ALLOWABLE (AGE 50 OR OLDER)
2006	$15,000	$20,000
2007	$15,500	$20,500
2008	$16,000	$21,000
2009	$16,500	$21,500

* After the year 2006, the maximum allowable contribution increases by an incremental $500 per year.

Here are a couple of tips for investing in your 401(k) or 403(b) plan:

- Set your contributions as a percentage of your earnings so, when you get a raise, you automatically end up contributing more money to the plan. You also end up saving more on your taxes, seeing as you are contributing more pretax dollars.
- Match your risk level in your plan with your comfort level and your lifestyle. For example, if you have a child, you might want to consider placing some of your money in safer investments for security reasons.

One additional thing you might want to note is if and when you change jobs, you don't have to cash out your company 401(k). Rather, you can roll this money into an IRA account, which is another tax-deferred retirement plan (more information on this type of account below). An IRA rollover saves you from paying the IRS the 10 percent early-withdrawal penalty and the deferred taxes on top of that. Dipping into your retirement savings, even when it's time to say "ta ta" to your employer, isn't a good idea because you lose the power of compound interest. Let's say you had $5,000 sitting in your 401(k) account, it would grow to $57,791.26 when that $5,000 is compounded over 30 years at 8.5 percent. If you withdraw that $5,000 now because you didn't set up an IRA rollover account when you changed jobs, you lose over $50,000 worth of compound interest. You can set up an IRA rollover account at your local bank, brokerage, or mutual fund company.

IRAs

You don't need to worry if your employer doesn't have a compensation package that includes a 401(k) or 403(b) plan. You can just as easily set up what is called an individual retirement account (IRA). You can get this type of account through your local bank, brokerage firm, or mutual fund company. You can even set it up online, or over the phone. Like a 401(k) or 403(b), an IRA is like a house—a house that needs decorating! An investor can fill that house with the types of "decorations" (investments) he or she wants— mutual funds, stocks, index funds, and more (see chapter 7). As with any real house, the decorations are chosen according to the tastes and needs of the owner. Some people like flashy things; others go for classic style; others still might prefer a mix. Whatever your taste, an IRA plan allows you to create a balanced portfolio to suit your needs and investment style. IRA accounts are also protected through the Federal Deposit Insurance Corporation (FDIC) up to $250,000. The Securities Investor Protection Corporation (SIPC) also offers insurance for investment accounts up to $500,000 (of which $100,000 can be cash), and covers your investments in stocks, bonds, mutual funds, insurance products, and other securities, which are not covered by the FDIC.

Traditional IRA versus Roth IRA

Choices, choices, choices. There are two types of IRAs you can sign up for—the traditional IRA and the Roth IRA (named after U.S. Senator William V. Roth Jr.). The main difference between the two is in the way you're taxed when you retire. The traditional IRA allows you to contribute pre-tax dollars (this works out through tax deductions). When contributing to a traditional IRA account, the tax advantage can appear in one of two forms depending on how much tax is withheld from your paycheck: a tax refund or a reduced tax bill. This plan can be very powerful because it reduces your taxable income and, therefore, the taxes you pay. However, when you begin withdrawing the money (you're required to withdraw your money once you reach the age of 70½), you then have to pay taxes on your contributions and on the money you've made in your investments. Once you hit retirement age, you're generally in a lower tax bracket than you are when you're in the workforce. So, theoretically you still end up paying less in tax when taking distributions from your IRA than you would have paid in ordinary income tax in your younger years if you hadn't contributed to a plan. Even though the future tax bill looks hefty, keep in mind, through the power of compound interest, your funds will have grown exponentially.

The Roth IRA is different than the traditional IRA in that you pay income tax on the money you contribute. Therefore, your contributions are not tax deductible. Assuming you're 59½ years old, and your account has been in existence for over five years, you can withdraw your money from this account at any time without being taxed. There are income limits on the Roth IRA. To make a maximum contribution of $4,000 (plus an additional $1,000 if you're over the age of fifty), as a single person, you have to earn less than $99,000 a year. As a couple filing a joint tax return, your limit is $156,000. The amount you can contribute is reduced gradually as your income increases, and then completely eliminated if your earnings reach $114,000 a year or $166,000 for couples filing a joint tax return.

What's Best?

Choosing between an IRA and a Roth IRA has everything to do with whether you want to pay taxes now or later. A young person typically has fewer financial commitments and earns a lower income—therefore, paying less in taxes. So, one school of thought is a young person should use a Roth IRA because that person doesn't benefit nearly as much from the tax reduction a traditional IRA provides. In addition, there is always the risk that taxes may increase in the future, depending on the government, its policies, and the status of Social Security funding. If taxes increase in the future, then a Roth IRA will be better for the investor seeing as the young investor will have already paid taxes on the dollars invested. Last, the Roth IRA allows you to grow your money compounded, whereas if you invest in a traditional IRA, you grow your money and the government's money compounded. In essence, you're doing the government a favor by growing money for them. Some experts believe if your time horizon for using your retirement funds is greater than 15 years, you get a bigger benefit from a Roth IRA than with a traditional IRA. It is also important to note that with a Roth IRA, your money grows tax-free meaning that you don't have to pay taxes on the growth and income generated by your investments the way you do in a traditional IRA. In the traditional IRA scenario, you're taxed after the growth, instead of before the growth occurs.

The opposite school of thought is that a young person should invest in a traditional IRA because, through the traditional IRA, it's easier to max out the annual contributions to the account. Investing in a traditional IRA means there are more dollars available to you for investment before you pay taxes on your income. Theoretically, if you wanted to invest the maximum ($4,000 per year) in a Roth IRA, you'd have to save approximately $5,700 in gross-income dollars because you'd have just paid approximately 30 percent of your income in taxes. Contributing the maximum to a traditional IRA is easier because you have more pretax dollars kicking around.

Can You Have It All?

If you cannot get a tax deduction on the traditional IRA because your employer covers you with their 401(k) plan, then you can also invest in the Roth IRA. A traditional IRA will be of little benefit to you in this scenario, because the taxable benefit will have already been used in the 401(k) plan. Juggling both of these plans tends to give you the best of both worlds—employers will sometimes match your contributions, free money, into the 401(k) plan with pretax dollars, *and* the Roth IRA means you save money in the future by paying taxes now rather than later.

You may think contributing $4,000 per year to an IRA account may not be enough to retire on. But remember the power of compound interest is great and will grow your contributions into a nice nest egg by the time you retire. Below is a list of the contribution limits each year for both the traditional and Roth IRAS.

YEAR	MAXIMUM ALLOWABLE (AGE 49 OR YOUNGER)	MAXIMUM ALLOWABLE (AGE 50 OR OLDER)
2006	$4,000	$5,000
2007	$4,000	$5,000
2008	$5,000	$6,000
2009	$5,500	$6,500

*** After the year 2008, the maximum allowable contribution increases by an incremental $500 per year.

If you are self-employed, you have access to IRA accounts with even larger contribution limits. These plans are called Simplified Employee Pension (SEP) IRAS. There is also a One-Person 401(k)/Profit-Sharing plan. You'll want to explore these options so you, too, can put your pretax dollars to good use!

So when should you start investing? Is it ever really too early to start thinking about retirement? Not really. Typically, people start investing in a 401(k) plan and IRAS when they get their first full-time job. However, nowadays, you can even set these types of plans up while working a part-time job. The easiest way to make retirement savings painless is to time your contributions with your paychecks. So, if you get paid once per month, ensure you contribute to your plan on that day. Similarly, if you get paid biweekly, set your contributions to match those days. Automating your contributions is a terrific idea—you won't have to worry about manually writing checks, and/or visiting your financial institution every time you get paid.

Saving for Your Kid's Education

The cost of education has increased by more than one hundred percent since the 1980s making it difficult for a parent, grandparent, or legal guardian to save. Thankfully, each state has a unique plan allowing you to contribute to your child's future educational costs. This includes the cost of tuition, books, and the like at most accredited two- and four-year university and college programs. In addition to this, the funds can also be used at some vocational, technical, and foreign schools. These savings plans are also referred to as 529 Accounts.

When you set up a 529 Account, whether your kid is one month old or eighteen years old, your child becomes the beneficiary of the money in the account rather than being the owner of the account. By being the beneficiary, a child will still have access to student loans when they attend post-secondary school, because the funds will not be directly linked to their Social Security number. The Uniform Transfers to Minors Act (UTMA) are alternatives to the 529 Account. In these accounts, the funds are linked to the child's Social Security number, thus posing a problem for them if they need to apply for student loans. However this account allows the parent or guardian control over the money until the child is eighteen years old, and it enables them to transfer ownership of property to their children. It is important to note that UTMA contributions are irrevocable gifts and automatically become the property of the beneficiary (which cannot be changed) when they reach the designated age of majority.

The benefits of investing in the 529 Account are you don't have to pay tax on the money when it's withdrawn from the account. In some states, you may even receive a tax deduction. As with a 401(k) and IRA, the contributor fills the "house" with the types of investments that suit the investor. Institutions providing the 529 Accounts often have choices of various packages, portfolios, or investment structures, which are matched to your child's age. The last and most powerful benefit you receive is your money grows through the power of compound interest, making it easier for you to reach your savings goals.

Every state has a limit on the amount of money that can be contributed each year. For tax purposes, you need to know you can contribute up to $11,000 per year, if you file a single tax return and $22,000 per year if you file jointly without paying a gift tax. You can contribute to your 529 Account automatically through deductions from your bank account and/or through the 401 Education Plan, which allows you to contribute right off your paycheck. The 401 Education Plan isn't very popular because there are lower limits to what you can contribute each year—$2,000.

If your child decides not to go to school, the money you've invested and the interest it has earned in the 529 Plan still belongs to you. To avoid the 10 percent government penalty for not using the funds for education, you can pass the savings along to another child. For more information on saving for your child's education check out www.savingforcollege.com.

Conclusion

You've embarked on a wonderful journey—a journey to better your financial knowledge. You now know more about investments, basic finance, and the tools to help you achieve your financial dreams, than you did when you picked up this book. You're well equipped to become rich by thirty!

Still, you may find yourself wondering where you go from here. You aren't alone. It's completely normal to be overwhelmed by so much information. So, if you find your head spinning, or if you're worried about losing your focus, concentrate on the following ten pieces of advice. They'll ensure you stay the course.

Ten Pieces of Advice

1. **Start now.** Whatever your financial situation may be, start to invest right now. Time is of the essence. The longer you wait, the less wealthy you'll become.

Think of it like this: by waiting, you're actually cheating yourself out of money. Start investing when you're young. You'll thank yourself later.

2. **Take control.** Healthy money management requires you learn to spend wisely, handle debt appropriately, and, sometimes, change your priorities. Use tools like realistic budgeting and planning to help you achieve your financial goals.

3. **If you don't need it, don't buy it!** Overspending can have an incredibly negative influence on your life. Couples who have spending problems, for example, are typically the first in line for a divorce! Overspending can spiral into debt and bankruptcy—and that affects every area of your life. You *can* control your spending! It just requires a change in your mindset.

4. **It doesn't matter what you have, it's what you do with it that counts.** You could be the poorest person on the block. You might only have $25 to save each month. You might only have $10! It doesn't matter. Do it! Don't be discouraged. There are thousands of very wealthy people who started with almost nothing. You can do it, too!

5. **Try mutual funds.** If you're looking for a relatively safe and easy way to maximize your return—even with a very small initial investment—mutual funds are the way to go. They allow you to get into the market, to diversify, and to contribute limited funds.

6. **Contribute regularly.** By contributing to your investment portfolio regularly, you get to take advantage of the average price over the long haul. You don't have

to worry about timing the market. Leave that to the experts.

7. **Diversify!** If you have all your eggs in one basket, and you drop that basket, all of your eggs are going to break. Diversify your investments to reduce your risks.

8. **Be patient.** Money grows exponentially over the long run. It doesn't necessarily grow immediately. Hang on for the ride. Markets change so much through time. They go up, and they go down. Try to see past the short-term fluctuations and focus on the long term. In the long term, knowing history tends to repeat itself, the markets are expected to perform with a return of 10 to 12 percent. Investors who focus on the short term tend only to make less than 4 percent. Figure out a strategy to suit your risk-tolerance level, and stick with it through thick and thin.

9. **Pay yourself first.** You need to balance your debt reduction with saving and investing. Don't concentrate on one area and ignore the other. Use the "debt reduction" technique outlined in chapter 4 to get rid of the debt that's holding you back, but always ensure you're saving some money, as well. Saving for your future should be the top priority on your personal budget.

10. **Strike a balance.** Don't forget the three principles of wealth: spend wisely, save and invest, and give back to your community. This last item can be achieved by volunteering, or by donating funds or goods to a charity. You'll feel good knowing you've done something positive for the community, and for yourself.

You can refer back to these pages whenever you need a refresher course, or just a little motivation. I also recommend you further enrich your knowledge of money management by continuing to learn and practice healthy money-management techniques. Check out my Web site, **www.richbythirty.com** for my personal newsletter, an excellent glossary of terms, and some good links to other financial sites.

Now get out there and get going!

Index